Things
ALL
YOUNG
ADULTS
Should Know

101 Things ALL YOUNG ADULTS Should Know

JOHN HAWKINS

RIVER GROVE
BOOKS

Published by River Grove Books
Austin, TX
www.rivergrovebooks.com

Distributed by River Grove Books

Design and composition by Greenleaf Book Group
Cover design by Greenleaf Book Group

Cataloging-in-Publication data is available.

Print ISBN: 978-1-63299-133-1

eBook ISBN: 978-1-63299-134-8

First Edition

Thank you to Bob and Ann Hawkins for being a great set of parents.
Thank you to Jewett and John Brown for being the best grandparents any young child could ever
want. Thank you to God for everything, especially for being born in a country like America.
Last but not least, thank you to my best friend, Tiffiny Ruegner, who always stuck by me.

TABLE OF CONTENTS

INTRODUCTION

One day you are going to be old. Well, if you're lucky. If you're not lucky, you could walk into an open manhole or end up getting some spectacular new disease named after you. There are worse ways to go, right?

Assuming that doesn't happen, you will reach middle age, you'll look back over your life, and you'll say, "I wish I knew as much at eighteen as I do today." Let's face it, if you're not saying that, it means you're either completely hopeless because you haven't learned anything or you have some sort of head trauma that prevents you from remembering anything. If it's the latter, you're borrowing this book, so buy it again.

Oh, I know what you're thinking. "Middle-aged? Me? It seems so far away—and most of the forty-year-olds I know have beer guts, the beginning of male pattern baldness, and soul-crushing jobs that at least distract them from what went wrong in their first marriages. Well actually, I *assume* that's what's going on with them because I don't pay enough attention to old people to care."

Fair point.

However—and this may shock you—every forty-year-old on planet Earth was once eighteen like you. Yes, really! Your dad, grandpa, the creepy old guys who walk through the locker room naked letting it all hang out because they don't care anymore—they were all young once.

Wait, am I depressing you? Does thinking about that upset you a little? Really, it's not so bad . . . or at least it doesn't have to be. I will tell you that as you get older, most of the problems you have in life will be a direct result of mistakes you made upstream. Those little choices you make today, so small, so tiny, so insignificant that you don't even notice them—they accumulate over the course of a lifetime.

All of it happens faster than you think. One day you're eighteen years old, graduating from high school. The next day you're getting your first job. Soon after, you're thinking about getting married. Next, in the blink of an eye, you're forty years old in the middle of a midlife crisis wondering whether you should have fulfilled your childhood dream of becoming a circus acrobat.

In retrospect, it's pretty easy to see where you went wrong. After all, you think you know everything at eighteen, except the stuff you don't know, which you're confident that you'll figure out when the time comes.

Being eighteen is not just an age, though; it's a mentality. The world is your oyster at that age. That's the message you get from music, from TV, from movies. You see all these people up on the silver screen who are your age, who look like they could be your friends, who are doing all these great things. Meanwhile, you feel young, vibrant, and almost invincible. Your whole life is in front of you, and it seems like there are infinite possibilities.

Getting older isn't quite like that. That's not to say it's bad. It's just different. The good news is that you know a lot more about life at forty than you did at twenty. Part of that is raw knowledge, but experience is irreplaceable. Deeply loving another human being, being the only person for miles in a forest, having a gun pointed at you, trying and succeeding, achieving dreams years in the making, doing things nobody else seemed to think you could do—some things you just have to feel if you want to truly know and understand. Still, if you're around long enough, you start to realize there are no magic bullets. When you're younger, you may think that if you had money, a big house, a beautiful woman, a dream vacation . . . if you could have thousands of people listening to you, could have this experience, talk to that person, do this thing, then everything would be *wonderful*.

The truth is that's all crap.

It reminds me of a coat I wanted when I was eighteen. It was leather with an American flag on the back, and I thought it was the most amazing thing I had ever seen. I couldn't afford the coat and that upset me so much, I kid you not, I got choked up and a tear rolled down my cheek. To me, that coat wasn't a coat; it was a representation of all the things I wanted that I couldn't have. Long story short, I got my heart's desire and . . . I didn't wear it all that often because it was leather and the city I was living in had mild winters. After a couple of years, someone stole the coat from my dorm room. I wasn't particularly happy about that, but I wasn't exactly broken up either. I certainly didn't make any move to go buy another coat. Today, when I think back about that coat, the first word that comes to mind is "cheesy."

This is what life is like. It always looks greener on the other side of the fence, no matter which side of the fence you're on. That's not to say that nothing will bring you pleasure long term in life, but be careful what you use to fill gaps inside you, because over time, no matter how permanent it seems, it will probably turn out to be a patch. That's why you'd better learn to like yourself and enjoy the day-to-day journey instead of reaching for a brass ring that's going to almost inevitably disappoint you in the end.

If you're twenty, all of this probably sounds perfectly awful or perhaps implausible. By the time you're forty, you're going to be on a yacht somewhere getting a massage from your hot spouse, thinking about your next vacation and how you're going to cure cancer while you're listening to the wonderful news about how a new cloning breakthrough will allow everyone to live until four hundred. I certainly hope that's how things turn out for you, but if you have a more conventional lifestyle at forty, remember that's not so bad either.

Once you get to this age, you know yourself better; you don't care as much what other people think of you; hopefully you won't have a spool or a couch you found on the side of the road in your living room; and you'll have enough experience to get a handle on life. Plus, there are a lot of rewards in life that go beyond what you're going to see at a party, drunk at a club at two a.m., or on MTV. Being middle-aged isn't the end of the good life; it's just another chapter of the book that will be the story of you one day.

Congratulations on being smart enough to think that far ahead or, alternately, being bored enough to finally read that book your parents gave you when you graduated from high school. This book won't provide all the answers to life's questions, but it will give you twenty years' worth of education in the school of hard knocks in just a few hours. Live it, learn it, love it—and it will change the course of your life forever.

Chapter 1

FRIENDSHIP

1. Be the one who moves first in social situations.

Unfortunately, whether you're talking about dates, friendly outings, parties, or just about any other type of social gathering you can imagine, most people have a tendency to wait for someone else to reach out to them.

There are a variety of reasons for this. Some people are shy and don't feel comfortable making the first move. Others fear rejection. Then there are the people who get so caught up in their routine that they hate to break it, even to do something fun. You also can't discount the people who aren't that social, lack confidence, or who forget how much they enjoy being with other people until they're out doing something.

What it all boils down to is that if you want to have a thriving social life, you need to accept that YOU are the one who has to make it happen.

That means with some friends, if you don't reach out to them, the friendship will die.

It means that if you aren't the one asking a woman out on a date (or at least being unsubtle in your flirting, ladies), then that date may never happen.

It means that if you aren't the one who suggests your friends go somewhere, then you may not be going anywhere.

Is that fair? No, it just is what it is.

As a practical matter, let me tell you what being social looks like.

When I go to political conventions and head out to dinner, I invite all the people I know who seem like they're entertaining. Sometimes that means twenty of us head out somewhere, sometimes it means six or seven of us, and on occasion, it means only three or four. It means that entertaining online friendships I maintained for years disappeared when I stopped reaching out. It means that out of every woman I ask on a date, maybe one out of three says "yes" and the other two beg off because they have to brush their hair that night. (Yes, I have really had a woman tell me that.)

Can that be a lot of hassle at times? Sure, but it also means that when I'm at conventions, people ask me where the parties are. It means I go on trips with friends. It means I'm fantastic at networking.

Do you have to do all that? Can't you be the friend who gets invited places? Sure, but remember, if you leave how social you're going to be to other people, you may end up spending a lot more time alone than you like.

2. Set hard boundaries in your personal life.

You ever wonder why a woman stays in a relationship with a man who hits her? Ever seen someone enable an alcoholic or drug addict who makes her life a living hell? Have you ever asked yourself why you put up with a "friend" who treats you like crap?

It's all about boundaries.

Human beings test each other's limits. It's just part of what we do—and in certain areas, some of us will go further than others. So what happens when someone who likes to push it to the limit runs up against another person who can't say "no?"

Yes, exactly.

To put it another way, people get treated as well or as badly as they allow themselves to be treated. That doesn't mean that people with boundaries don't ever get treated poorly; it means they don't allow it to continue.

Take the first example of a woman who has a man hitting her. I've known women who have put up with that *for years*. I also knew a woman who dumped a guy she had been dating for years because he got angry and shoved her once. They were both attractive, intelligent, likable women, but there was one big difference. One of them had a firm boundary and the other one didn't.

Want to know why someone in your life treats you like absolute garbage? It's because you allow him to do it. There are plenty of guys who will dump a woman without a second thought for cheating on them, and plenty of women who will end a relationship if they hear the c-word drop.

So, knowing that, what are you going to allow in your life? Are you willing to lose respect for yourself to keep someone in your life? Are you okay with being abused because you don't want to be "mean" enough to tell someone to stop? How important is your happiness?

There are some people you just don't screw with because you know they're not putting up with your BS. Take it from me, it's good to be one of those people.

3. You will become like the people you spend the most time with.

I'm sure you've heard someone say, "Birds of a feather flock together," but a quote that may be even more apt is, "A good friend will help you move, a great friend will hire you a lawyer, but a true friend will help you hide the body."

Here's a pro tip: You don't want to have friends who ask you for help hiding a body. You may laugh, but the prisons are full of people who broke the law because they didn't want to disappoint their friends and ended up in jail because of it. You hang out with friends who get drunk out of their minds every weekend, use drugs, curse, or who are just a-holes, and you will probably do the same thing because you don't want to disappoint your pals.

We like to tell ourselves that we're "set apart" and can't be easily influenced. That's a load of bullshit. There are corporations you care nothing about that pay millions of dollars to get their ad in front of you for thirty seconds because they *know* they can change your behavior, but you think friends you like and spend hours with can't influence you? Of course they can!

So ask yourself some tough questions about your friends. Would you introduce these people to your parents? Do they have good character? Are they people you'd trust in an emergency, which hopefully would not involve moving a dead body?

Most of all, are these people you want to be like? If the answer is "no," you should ask yourself some questions about whether these people are ones you want to spend a lot of time with.

Don't get me wrong; everyone has different strengths and weaknesses. If we cut people loose for not being perfect, we wouldn't have any friends; however, don't wave off the fact that your friends help shape who you are as a human being. If your friend is a liar or a thief or a junkie, you're more likely to be that way too if you hang out with him long term.

Choose your friends wisely because they aren't only your friends; they're people who have an outsized influence on who you're going to become as a person.

4. Don't loan money to your friends.

I'm not talking about a "Hey, I forgot my wallet, spot me $5 until tonight" sort of loan; I'm talking about a "The rent's due and I'm broke. Can you help me out? I swear I'll pay you next week!"

Why shouldn't you loan your friends money?

For the simplest reason in the world: you'd like to continue to be their friend.

Let me explain: Most of the time when people ask you for money, it's because they're terrible with money in the first place. That's why they don't have any. They're in an apartment or car they can't afford, they drank the rent money, they bought some shoes instead of paying the power bill, or they have too much lifestyle for their salary. The other people who end up asking you for money are the people who don't have any in the first place. Either they have a lousy job and a lot of bills or, alternately, they've lost their job and haven't found another. Those two groups encompass 99 percent of the people who'll ask you for money outside of outright hustlers.

Of course, people don't admit to that. They come to you and tell you they had some "unexpected bills" and just need to get over the hump and then you'll get paid as soon as their paycheck comes in, they swear!

But think this through: If someone is terrible with money or is flat broke, how likely is she to have enough money to take care of her bills *and* have enough to pay you back?

Not likely.

Then what's going to happen when you don't get paid back?

You're going to get *huffy*. She *promised* to pay you back. Where's *your money?* She *owes* it to you! Meanwhile, the person you loaned the money to begins to see you as one more jerk hassling her for cash, like the power company and the phone company. However, they can cut off the power and disconnect the phone, while you can only give dirty looks; so who's getting paid first?

This is not a situation you want to get into. So tell your friend the truth: Sorry, but you don't loan money. Yes, you understand his situation is different, but you don't loan money. Sure, you know he needs it, but you can't help him because you don't loan anyone money.

Alternately, if you have the money to spare and your friend is really in need, then here's an idea: Give it to him. Over the years, I've bought two weeks' worth of groceries for friends. I've bought Christmas presents for another friend's kids. Those weren't loans; they were gifts. I was glad to give them, my friend was glad to receive them, and we had no friend-ship-wrecking expectations that I would ever be paid back. Is that a good idea? A bad idea? Well, let's put it this way: at least you'll still be friends when it's over. You can't necessarily say the same thing after a loan.

5. "It's not what you know; it's who you know." Use that to your advantage when you can.

I have metal business cards. They're heavy, they look fantastic, and typi-cally, they stand out from every other business card that people get at an event. They also cost a little over $2 each.

Why would I pay so much for a business card? Because I want to make an impression—and I do. People often "ooh" and "aah" over the cards; they remember that I had a metal business card years later and most impor-tantly, the cards give the impression that I must be somebody important and worth knowing, or else why would I have a metal business card?

Along similar lines, even though I've never been particularly big on holidays, I typically send out personalized Christmas cards to friends, fam-ily, important business associates, and people I want to get to know better. It's a personal touch that gives people the impression that you're friendly, and it sticks with them.

Even though I genuinely dislike air travel, there was a time when I was going to five or six political conventions a year, and when I did, I met every person I could, handed out business cards, invited people to dinner, and went to parties left and right. Why? It helps build that personal con-nection. When people have talked to you in person, shaken your hand, or better yet, gone to dinner with you, they tend to be well inclined toward you. They pick up the phone when you call, they respond to your emails, and if you need a small favor, they tend to grant it.

Do you think people go to schools like Harvard and Yale for the education? No, they go to those schools for the contacts and because a "Yale man" is likely to do well and is more willing to help another "Yale man." You might not be able to go to Yale, but can you go to church? Can you make a good impression on your boss's wife at the company picnic?

Some people don't think it's worth it to do all of this, and then they wonder why someone who's dumber, uglier, and less talented is getting opportunities they'd kill for while they're stuck in neutral. Why does it seem like people are falling all over themselves to give Prince Charming whatever he wants while everyone treats you like Prince Schmuck? It's because Charming took the time to build relationships with people and it paid off, while you didn't bother. When people know you and like you, they will look for ways to help you out. You need that in your life.

As an introvert who once had poor people skills, I know this isn't easy-peasy for everyone. It can feel *intimidating* to walk up and introduce yourself or to glad-hand your way around the room. Furthermore, if you're an introvert, it can tire you out because talking to people may take energy from you instead of hype you up like it would an extrovert. So read some books about communication, get in some practice, and start meeting some people who can help you get ahead in life!

6. Think twice before telling anyone to end a relationship.

When you have friends in relationships, inevitably some of them are going to go bad. They're going to be miserable, they're going to fight all the time, their partner is going to cheat on them, and they're going to tell you stories that make you go, "What the hell is going on with these people?"

When you're thinking, "I'd rather dig my eyes out with a rusty spoon than put up with the crap they're dealing with," it's tempting to tell them to break it off.

But unless you're talking about someone whose life is in danger, you're better off keeping your opinion to yourself.

Why?

Because people have a tendency to slant and exaggerate what's happening in a relationship. When they're telling you that their husband cheated on them, they don't tell you that they've been having their own affair and haven't slept with him in two years. Your friend tells you that his girlfriend screamed at him for ten minutes, but not that she barely left his side for three weeks when he was in the hospital a few months ago after a car wreck. He doesn't want to tell you that his "crazy" fiancée is the only woman in his entire life he's dated for more than a week.

Even setting that aside, people have different tastes, standards, and levels of self-esteem. In your mind, it's *obvious* they could find someone better, but they don't believe it. You find a cheating boyfriend to be intolerable, while they think all men cheat. You don't get why he doesn't try the single life for a while, but he's terrified to be alone.

So, what happens when you start encouraging your friend to dump their horrible partner? Well, if she decides to stay with him, suddenly she's going to feel uncomfortable because she's going to feel like she has to choose between you and her boyfriend. If she dumps the guy and gets back together with him again later, she's still going to be uncomfortable with you. Even if they do break up, what if she regrets it six months down the road when she sees him making out with somebody new in the corner of some club? She might say it out loud and she might not, but she's going to remember that you were the one pushing her to dump the guy she wants right now.

More importantly, you're not the one who has to live with the ramifications of a breakup; they do. It's pretty common to date someone, realize they're not right for you, but still have a powerful attraction toward them years later because they scratched an itch deep down in your soul.

Do you really want to risk a friendship by getting in the middle of something like that?

So, ask hard questions. Feel free to tell your friend that what's happening isn't good, isn't normal, and is something they shouldn't tolerate . . . but don't tell them they need to cut their partner loose. Ultimately, it's their decision and you should let them make it and live with the consequences.

Chapter 2

LOVE

7. There's a right time, a right place, and a right person to have sex with.

We live in a sex-drenched society. We hear about it in music; we see it on TV; it's used to sell us products. It has become so ever present that we barely even bat an eye when it's shoved in our faces. It has become so over-the-top that you almost feel like if you're not having sex right this second, you're missing out.

Now, I could come at this morally and tell you that ideally, you shouldn't have sex until marriage. While that's true, there are a lot of people who aren't going to listen to advice, so let's set morals aside and talk about sex—if you're going to have sex.

First of all, men and women both like sex, but they have different incentives. Men are never going to get pregnant. They don't ever have to worry about a woman raping them. They get high fives from their friends when they have sex instead of being called a slut. Because of this, men tend to have a much more casual attitude about sex. Not all men will admit this, but most of them are okay with casual sex and "friends with benefits" arrangements. Women, not so much, although I will tell you that there are an awful lot of respectable, buttoned-down married women who went through a "promiscuous stage." Maybe they went on vacation and had sex with two or three different guys, spent a few months going to bars and picking up men, or went through a *lot* of short-term sexual relationships for a year or two. If you're a woman, it's never hard to find a willing guy, and if your friends don't find out about it, it can be tempting to live out those sexual fantasies for a while.

The reason women stop doing this is the same reason most men would get bored with casual sex if they could get laid as easily as women. A lot of times, sex with a new partner is not that great or it's just flat-out awkward. Plus, sex is an intimate experience. When you share that with someone who turns out to be annoying, scary, or crazy, it doesn't feel good. Also, if the sex is good, you're enjoying someone's company, and suddenly she just decides to move on, it hurts. Maybe it shouldn't because you knew what you were getting into, but it does. It also doesn't nurture you as a human being the same way a loving relationship does. That's unfortunate because many people use meaningless sex as a substitute for a relationship, but it's a poor replacement for the real thing.

Men in particular have trouble with this concept because, unlike women, they can't simply pick any person they're interested in, flirt a little bit, and have her ready to spend the night in bed. So, many men spend their whole lives wanting and never getting the sort of casual sex spree even an average-looking woman can have at her leisure anytime she wants. Let me tell you this, guys: if you were getting all the sex you wanted right now, 98 percent of you would be tired of it in six months. There's a reason most rock stars, actors, and pro athletes who are absolutely drowning in attractive women give it all up to get married. The reality is a lot emptier than the fantasy.

Getting beyond that to sex in relationships, it's important for women to take their time before having sex with a guy they're dating. There are two important reasons for that. First off, as I've already noted, there are a lot of guys who are just interested in sex, and some of them will lie to you to get it. That's *always* going to be a risk for you; however, the other danger is that if you sleep with a man too soon, he may legitimately not realize he's not that into you. You have a nice conversation with a little making out on the first date, watch a movie and make out on the second date, and then sleep with the guy on the third date, and the honest truth is, this guy still has no idea in the world if you two are compatible over the long haul. He'll still have sex with you if he can, but he also may disappear shortly thereafter. Will he feel bad about it? If he's a good guy, a little bit, but typically men don't get as attached as women after sex. They're also generally not as good at handling emotions; taking off may look more attractive to a man than dealing with your tears and anger if he tells you he's just not feeling it anymore soon after the two of you bumped uglies in the backseat of his car.

Then there's married sex. First off, I'm not excusing anybody who cheats on his partner. That's wrong. But I'm also going to tell you that nobody gets married so he can not have sex. If you're not servicing your partner for whatever reason, at some point you should expect him or her to break and cheat on you. I'm not excusing it or saying it's okay, but sex is part of your marital duties, and if you don't fulfill them, don't be surprised or absolve yourself of blame if your partner eventually finds someone else who will.

Again, even if you set aside moral issues, it's a really bad idea to cheat on your partner. You may not get caught—at first—but chances are, down the road, you're going to slip up. Additionally, once you start cheating, it's going to be difficult to voluntarily become faithful again because that outside relationship is going to be filling a need you should be getting in your marriage. Wouldn't it be better to work it out with your partner rather than look outside the marriage? If the answer to that question is "no," then wouldn't you be better off trying to work toward the most amicable divorce possible rather than creating a train wreck down the line that will still probably lead to a divorce?

One last piece of advice: Be cautious about dating people who are separated or getting divorced. There are so many potential pitfalls. For one thing, people coming out of bad marriages are often emotionally wounded and unpredictable. It doesn't matter how well things seem to be going; the aftermath of that previous marriage may tear your relationship apart. Also, people who are in that situation are often not scrupulously honest about what's going on in their relationship. If they're interested in you, they have every incentive to tell you that their previous relationship is over, they have no feelings for the other person, and they're handling it well. Seldom is that true. A bad marriage is a traumatic event, and most people will need months or even years to get over it.

Long story short, sex in the real world isn't like it is on the big screen. Even if you don't get an STD or get pregnant, there are a lot of pitfalls you can run into. Think about that before you end up naked with someone for the first time.

8. Make yourself happy first.

Don't be one of those men who loses his own identity because he gives up everything, including his own happiness, to try to make his marriage work. Don't be the woman who bends over backward to be her child's friend and wonders how she ended up raising such a little monster. Don't be the father who spends twenty years working sixty hours a week at a job he hates to take care of his family, only to be shocked when his wife takes the kids and demands a divorce because he's never at home.

Set some boundaries, choose yourself first, and refuse to give up your own happiness for anyone else.

For people who are service oriented, this may be a tough concept to swallow. For others, it may sound a little selfish. What kind of person thinks of making herself happy *before* her husband, children, or parents? I'll tell you which people think of making themselves happy *before* other people: the happy ones.

That's not only because you know what makes you happy, but also because *nobody* cares as much about your happiness as you do. If you don't make yourself happy, you certainly shouldn't expect anyone to do it for you. Additionally, how are you going to make someone else happy if you're unhappy? Sure, you might be able to grit your teeth and do it for a while, but if you're not happy yourself, you'll soon come to resent it.

On the other hand, if you're happy and your needs are taken care of, it's easy to do nice things for other people. This is what people who become so "selfless" that they make themselves miserable forget. When you're unhappy, you're less pleasant, patient, understanding, and kind. Is that the "you" that should be around your kids? Your husband? At work? With your friends? Great job, Johnny Crabapple! Everybody loves the bitter, short-tempered ass who always thinks his sacrifices are unappreciated. Do you want that to be you? Really? *Really?*

9. Women and men are looking for different reactions when they tell you their problems.

Women and men are different, very different—and I'm not just talking about the plumbing. "Low maintenance" for a woman means she has more emotional issues than 90 percent of guys. Women tend to spend hours analyzing why you were so quiet today when you were too sleepy to make good conversation.

However, the biggest difference between the way men and women think is the way they deal with problems. When a man starts talking to you about a problem in his life, he's looking for a potential solution. The boss doesn't think he delegates enough authority? Then how can he delegate more? He needs to regularly sleep until early morning but wakes up when the sun shines in his windows? Get blackout curtains. He wants to bring a woman over to his house for dinner but doesn't know what to cook? Sure, a steak and potato will be fine! Identify the problem, come up with a solution, and then watch the football game to celebrate a job well done.

This is not how it works with women. When a woman starts telling you about the annoying biddy at work, the problems she has with her kid, or how her boss is getting on her case, she wants you to pay attention and make her feel heard. Men have trouble with this concept because they feel like they should offer up a solution and move on to other topics. After all, that's exactly how it works with other guys—except when a man tries that with a woman, he's soon puzzled when the woman says she doesn't feel like he's listening. Of course he listened! He even helped out by offering up a solution. What? Does the woman just want to sit there and marinate in her problem without making any effort to deal with it?

Yes, she does. Suck it up and deal with it, guys, or next thing you know, the woman will be telling you that she's "fine," but she'll sound really mad when she says it. You know what that means—right, guys? Okay, maybe you don't. It's bad!

Meanwhile, ladies, cut your man a little slack. He's trying to help. If he's a good guy and you're his woman, he wants to help you, to take care of you, to fix your problems, and to help make you happy. He views that as part of his job, and you should be glad that he feels that way. It shows that he's a good man and he cares about you. There's a lot to be said for that.

10. People are what they are and are probably not going to change much once they've reached adulthood.

The woman who cheats on her husband with you would probably cheat on you if you were to marry her. The woman who would be a perfect wife if she weren't so negative or was better with money isn't going to change because you tie the knot. The guy who hits you today will probably still hit you five years from now if you're still together.

People are what they are for a reason, and rarely does love, a good talking-to, a reluctant trip to a counselor, or the gift of a book change them.

It's important to understand this because throughout your life, you're going to run into people who are amazing . . . except for this one thing. He's so much fun to hang out with except that he's an alcoholic and he's a monster when he drinks. She's the most caring woman you've ever known, but every so often she has a mental breakdown and gets depressed for weeks at a time and threatens to kill herself. He'd be perfect if he were thinner. She'd be a great girlfriend if she didn't have all those sexual hang-ups.

Not everything is that big either.

Maybe you like hanging out with a friend but she has the awful habit of giving you long, detailed descriptions of what she does each day that are so dull you want to dig your eyes out with a spoon. Maybe your buddy is great to hang out with but he always claims to have forgotten his wallet every time you need to pay a bill. Maybe you're dating a woman who's fun to be around but is so crude that you're afraid she'll introduce herself to your mother by saying, "It's f****** great to meet you, Mom!"

The key thing to keep in mind is that people do change, but they do it in their own time, for their own reasons. That's why you can hope for change, you can encourage change, you can communicate that you want change, but there are never any guarantees that it will happen.

So, if there are things another person is doing that you don't like, you need to ask yourself if you can live with that person "warts and all." Are the positives you get from that person worth dealing with the negatives? If the answer is "yes," it makes things a little easier because you can remind yourself that you signed up for this when he's doing whatever it is that annoys you. Furthermore, if you do accept people as they are and hang in there long enough, you *may* get the changes you want when that person is ready for it.

On the other hand, if their problems are too big, too ugly, or too dangerous for you to deal with, then I hate to say it, but it's time to cut your losses. This is hard for some people to do, so they tend to stay mired in an intolerable situation over the long term, hoping desperately that everything will magically get better one day.

That does happen on occasion. Of course, people also win the lottery on occasion. How much of your life are you willing to give up waiting for that miracle to occur? Incidentally, there's no right answer to that question because every situation is different. The important thing is to go into it with your eyes open instead of hoping and praying that the other person will change.

11. Here's how to tell if someone is flirting with you.

When I was a teenager, I was hopeless with women because I was completely unable to read them. I can still remember not once, but *twice* making jokes about going on dates with attractive girls, having them express interest, and then waving them off. I once had a girl *grab my ass* and I told myself that it was probably an accident. Years after high school, I found out that a girl I had a huge crush on also had a huge crush on me. At the time, I would have been incredibly excited to date her, but I didn't have the slightest idea she was interested.

The problem for me was that I didn't have a lot of female friends, I didn't get how women thought, and I didn't understand how to read the signals women were sending. They were doing their part to make their interest in me known; I just couldn't see it. And because I couldn't see it, I was incredibly timid and, yes, even fearful in dealing with women.

What attractive women don't understand is that until guys understand how the dating world works, a beautiful woman is almost like a celebrity. She's the desirable one, and a guy has to approach her and risk rejection to get her attention, which she may give or wave off depending on her mood. If she's not interested, that rejection may feel *very* personal, like your value as a human being has been questioned.

However, guys, let me tell you, once you start meeting beautiful women, you know what you find? They're ordinary human beings who happen to be attractive. They have problems, flaws, fears, and insecurities like everyone else, and in fact, they sometimes have personalities that need a little work because they're so desirable that they've been able to get a lot of what they want because of their looks.

So, all that being said, how do you tell if another person is interested in you? Well, with men it's relatively easy.

Ladies, if a single man seeks you out, talks to you, and seems to enjoy your company, he probably wants to date you or, at the very least, sleep with you. Most women don't believe this, but it's true. That cute guy at the office who comes by your cubicle to chat every day? Uh-huh. Your male "best friend" whom you tell about other guys you go on dates with? Yep. Your female friend's brother who keeps encouraging you to come over and hang out? That's right.

Now, the bad news, ladies, is that I cannot tell you whether these guys want to date you or just want to sleep with you. Also, because of the fear of rejection, many men will approach and chat with women they're interested in without *ever* asking them out. Despite that, what I am telling you is that they're interested. They might laugh it off, they might deny it, and nothing may ever come of it, but they're checking you out. Do with that information what you will.

Because women are both more social and more subtle than men, it's not as simple to gauge their interest. What you usually end up having to do is watch for a large number of different signals to see if they happen in clusters. One or two of these signals may be an indication that she's interested, or she may just be friendly. If you see a large number of them, then she's probably on board with you. So, does she deliberately touch you for any reason? More importantly, if you touch her hand, arm, or shoulder, does she touch you back? Does she ask you questions about yourself? Does she ask if you're dating anyone? Does she laugh uproariously at your jokes? Does she look for excuses to be around you? Does she mirror your gestures? Put another way, if your arms are crossed or your chin is on both hands, does she do the same thing? Does she hold your stare or, alternately, look down instead of away to break eye contact? Does she find an excuse to tell you that she's single? Does she play with her hair in your presence?

If you're interested in a woman and she starts displaying a lot of these behaviors, go for it! Most women are flattered to be respectfully asked out, and if she doesn't bite, she'll probably politely turn you down or give you some lame excuse. Take it from someone who has been turned down more than a few times: it's not so bad. When a woman isn't interested in me, I assume there's a problem with her. So I don't take it personally. You shouldn't either, because it's not personal. She doesn't know the real you, just like you don't know the real her.

If she's not interested—or, ladies, if he's not, don't sweat it. Just move on to the next one and, if need be, the next one. Keep doing that long enough and you may find the person you spend the rest of your life with.

12. Take enough time to get to know a person before committing to them.

Love is not just an emotion; it's a chemical response in your body. It's dopamine, norepinephrine, and serotonin flooding through your body as you look at a woman and think, *There's no one I'd rather be with and no place I'd rather be than right here, right now with her—watching Andy Griffith reruns.* Then, something deep down inside of you goes, *Wait, I'd rather be here than at the fifty-yard line of the Super Bowl? I'd rather make out with her than have the five hottest celebrity women I know taking turns and using me as their personal sex slave? Okay, she just called me "Pookie Bear" and . . . and I'm okay with it. What the hell is going on here?*

Welcome to love . . . and love, particularly romantic, emotional love, is a beautiful, amazing, incredible thing—while it lasts. Sometimes it can last for quite a long time—for six months, a year, three years, and in a few cases, a lifetime. However, in most cases, that powerful, overwhelming emotional state is replaced with a different kind of love—the sort you build over time by getting to know someone, finding things you like about him or her, sharing experiences, and building an emotional connection. This is also a beautiful, amazing, incredible thing, and over the long haul, this is the sort of love that holds people together.

On the other hand, relationships that seem great and then quickly implode are often based on the first type of love. It can be a shocking experience. You're out of your mind over a woman. You think she's gorgeous, she's the woman you're most sexually attracted to, you can't spend enough time with her—but she also has a few flaws. She semiregularly picks fights with you for no good reason; she often tells you long, dull stories about her day; she gets incredibly jealous even though you're not even looking at another woman; she starts planning out your wedding two months into your relationship, and . . . *Oh my god*, what were you thinking? How did you end up with this girl? It gets so bad, you want to stop the car, get out, and *run*!

This is what people mean when they say that love is blind. It blinds you to the other person's faults, and before you can commit to a person and feel like he's the right one for you, you need a little time for some of that shine to rub off of him so you can look at him with a clear head that isn't totally controlled by your heart. That's why, ideally, you should wait at least three months before forsaking all other partners and settling for one person. Sure, your new boyfriend may *seem* great, but is that the chemicals talking? Give yourself a chance to find out.

That's even more applicable to marriage, and I could tell so many stories about women I know who got married too quickly and paid the price. I know *three different women* who ended up marrying either alcoholics or drug addicts who were completely unaware their partner used any sort of mood-altering substance. How could that possibly happen, especially to smart women? Well, again, love is blind.

You don't want to get divorced, and you *really* don't want to be the woman who marries a man despite having serious doubts about him who then gets divorced later. Take your time, be patient, and it may keep you from making a horrible mistake that will emotionally scar you for the rest of your life.

13. Men should embrace their masculinity, and women should embrace their femininity.

One of the biggest complaints I've heard from my female friends over the years is that men have gotten way too wimpy for their tastes. These women are looking for John Wayne types, and they keep running into pale, wishy-washy slackers who seem so emasculated that women question whether they have hormone issues.

If you're a man, are you decisive? Does your girl feel safe with you? Can she count on you to handle tough situations? Can you shoot a gun? Get rid of a spider in the house? Can you throw a punch? Are you comfortable being in charge? Are you chivalrous? Do you have a firm handshake? Are you someone people would want around during a crisis? If you're a man, these are things you should aspire to be.

Why be masculine if you're a man? Well, not only do women like it but men respect it, and believe it or not, it feels good.

For women, especially women who have jobs that force them to take on traditionally masculine roles, it can be easy to lose touch with your femininity. Are you feminine?

Would other people describe you as girly? Are you okay with letting a man you trust and care about help you with problems? Can you be vulnerable in front of a man? Are you okay with wearing your hair longer, putting on a dress, and rocking some heels? Is it possible for you to enjoy taking care of a man you care about?

Some women confuse femininity with being subservient to a man or have gotten so used to competing with men during their workday that the whole process feels awkward.

However, just as women tend to like masculine men, men tend to like feminine women. Furthermore, many women find that being feminine feels good. That's doubly true if you're a tough woman who's used to being in charge who finds a man so strong that she feels comfortable being feminine in his presence.

Life is not a one-size-fits-all situation, but rarely will you find a man who doesn't benefit from being able to display masculinity or a woman who doesn't make her life better by being feminine.

14. Learn to say, "I love you," "I was wrong," and "I apologize."

Supposedly, men are reluctant to ask for directions, but it's a lot harder to say "I love you, "I apologize," or "I was wrong." Ladies, you don't get off easy here either because you might be a little more comfortable with saying "I love you," but the other two phrases seem to be as tough for you as for the fellas.

"I love you" is an important phrase, and it's not something you drop too soon. If you're almost to the end of a nice first date and you hear an "I love you," your first instinct will probably be to run, and as I say elsewhere in the book, trust your instincts.

Once you're to the point where an "I love you" is appropriate, don't hesitate to say it. Tell your wife, your kids, and your parents that you love them all the time. If you're not used to saying it, it may seem a little strange at first, but it's important. More than a few times in my life, I've seen a marriage crumble because the man is working so hard to take care of his wife and kids that he forgets to be a loving husband and father. Then one day, the wife packs her suitcases, gets the kids, and leaves, telling him something like, "I don't think you even love me anymore." The man is flabbergasted because he's been working so hard because he does love his family. Don't they know? No, they don't. You have to tell them.

Besides, life is uncertain. Your parents could drop dead any day. Your son could get hit by a bus. Your wife could die in an airplane crash. If that happens, don't you want to at least look back and say, "At least she knew I loved her because I told her all the time"?

For some people, "I was wrong" and "I apologize" can be even tougher to say because they treat it as an admission of weakness. Instead, they'd rather have a long argument where they know they're wrong, the person they're talking to knows they're wrong, but they refuse to say it. It takes a big man to admit he's wrong, so don't be small. Instead of being the guy who gets on everyone's nerves because he can't admit the obvious, end the argument by saying "I was wrong" and/or "I apologize." It doesn't mean you lost, it means you're a reasonable human being.

"I love you," "I was wrong," and "I apologize" are powerful words. They can save marriages, deepen friendships, and change lives. Don't be afraid to use them!

15. The mother test.

Ladies, if there were a way to see how your future husband would treat you, would you be interested in knowing what that is? Guys, if you could find out what your future wife will be like, would you want to know about it? It's like finding out the future without having to pay $50 to some creepy lady pretending to be a gypsy who wants to read your palm.

Well, there is such a test. It's called the mother test, and it works slightly differently for each sex.

Ladies, watch how your boyfriend talks about his mother and pay great attention to how he treats her. Does he treat her like a queen or an annoyance? Is he respectful or disrespectful? Does he think the world of her or does he seem to find her aggravating, even when she's doing something nice for him?

Keep in mind that a man's mother is usually the first woman he truly loves. If he treats her poorly, don't expect to be treated much differently once the hot romance has cooled down and you've settled into your married life.

For men, it works a little differently. When you meet a woman's mother, you're meeting the closest thing to her genetically unless she has a twin. You're also getting an opportunity to be around the woman who shaped her environment growing up.

For good or ill, she's likely to share a lot of thought processes, character traits, and flaws with this woman. Also, because they share many of the same genetic traits, she's likely to age a lot like her mother. If you want to know what your wife will look like in thirty years, Mom's probably a good approximation.

Granted, you do have to take all of this with a grain of salt. If Mom's a raging alcoholic, it might explain why her son has a bad relationship with her. Also, if Mom's an alcoholic and because of that, her daughter doesn't drink it all, she's not likely to become an alcoholic. But, if Mom's an alcoholic, how does her child react to it? Does the son deny she has a problem? Does the daughter also tend to drink too much? Is he trying to get his mom to go to AA, or is her alcoholism never discussed openly? When you see those family dynamics, suddenly a lot of things going on in your own relationship may start to make sense for the first time.

There is a reason people say, "The apple doesn't fall far from the tree." It's because usually, it doesn't. When it does, it's almost always because people made a conscious decision to do things differently than their family did growing up. So, if you're horrified by the way your boyfriend treats his mother or by the way your girlfriend's mother behaves while she's okay with it, each has flunked the mother test. That's a red flag the size of a dinosaur, and if you ignore it, don't be surprised if you regret it down the road.

Chapter 3

SOCIAL SITUATIONS

16. Be nice until it's time to not be nice.

Yes, yes, I stole that line from *Road House*. Can you blame me? It's genius! It's also a philosophy worth living your life by. Don't take it from me; take it from the 1st Marine Division. Its motto is *No better friend, no worse enemy*.

As to the "be nice" part, it pays to treat other people well even if you don't have to do it. I remember an engineer who was a coworker. He was incredibly talented, but he was also a crusty jerk nobody wanted to deal with. Fortunately for him, he was so good that people had to pretend like his cranky "I got two hours of sleep and haven't had coffee yet" all-the-time personality didn't bother them . . . until the company came to the conclusion that it could get by without him. Even though he was the best guy in the room, he was still right out the door because nobody liked him.

There's another guy I know who owns his own business. He's a hard worker, an honest-to-goodness Einstein-level genius, and an amazing salesman. This is the sort of guy who could be rich, famous, and powerful . . .

except he can't get along with anybody else. He's so difficult to work with, he can't hold on to any top-of-the-line talent. He's such an ass that he ends up killing off business relationships that could make him millions. If he had a different personality, the world would be his oyster, but despite everything he has going for him, all of his potential is being wasted because he can't be nice to people.

On the other hand, when some people run across someone "nice," they immediately think "sucker." You give people like that an inch and not only will they take it a mile, they'll drag you along behind them the whole way. When you're dealing with people like that, there's something beautiful about watching their stunned reaction when they find out there's an iron fist under that velvet glove. Moreover, other people get to profit from their example.

If you know someone who's a great guy but you really don't want to **** with him, then most people will try to stay on his good side. That's human nature and you can make it work for you.

The key is to understand that balance. If you're a "nice guy" who doesn't ever want anyone to get mad at him, then you'll be treated like a patsy. If you're a jerk who flies off the handle at the slightest provocation, most people won't want to be around you. If you can combine the two and "be nice until it's time not to be nice," you'll have a lot of success in dealing with people long term.

17. If you want to know what a person really believes, look to their actions.

Life is full of people who say one thing and do another: the politician who says one thing before he's elected and does something else after; the product that's big on promises and short on delivery; the girl who says she's so into you but is somehow never available when it's time to go on a date.

To give you a real-world example, a friend of mine had a dent in her car. Two men walked up to her in a parking lot and offered to fix the dent for only $20. Sounds like a great deal, right? So, she agreed. The men then slammed a screwdriver through the dent, pulled it out, filled in the hole with a white substance, and then promptly asked for $50. My friend refused to pay them more, which was wise, because it turned out the "white substance" they used to fill the screwdriver hole was toothpaste. That's what happens when you pay attention to what people say and not what they've done.

It doesn't matter whether you're talking about Nigerian princes, politicians, or your relatives; the proof is in the pudding.

Worse yet, not only will people lie to you, they'll lie to themselves. That alcoholic really does plan to stop drinking; he just never does it. The guy who borrows money from you does mean to pay you back; he just doesn't. Your friend who's always late means to be on time; he just isn't.

That's why people say, "Money talks and bullcrap walks." It's also where phrases like "all hat and no cattle" come from.

Then there's the advice you get.

Over the course of your lifetime, you will have thousands of people trying to tell you how the world works. You'll have poor people telling you how to make money, fat guys telling you how to get in shape, and single women trying to tell you how to make your marriage work.

Don't pay any attention to what people say they're *going to do*; pay attention to what they've done. If you want to know what people are *really* about, watch what they *do*, not what they say. People's words will often lead you astray. Their track records seldom do.

18. Learning to really listen to people will change your relationships for the better.

When I was young, I wasn't very good with people. I didn't have a lot of friends. I wasn't dating. I didn't get invited to parties. The more unpopular

I became, the more I tried to come up with funny or cool things to say. Unfortunately, when you're talking too much it doesn't come across all that well. It turns funny into "goofy," and "cool" into "trying too hard."

That's when I learned a single lesson that revolutionized the way I interacted with people. Instead of focusing on what I was going to say, I started listening to what the other person was saying. I nodded my head to keep them talking. I asked relevant follow-up questions that showed I was paying attention . . . and it changed everything.

Why?

Because unless you're a rock star, celebrity, or pro athlete, almost everyone is more interested in hearing themselves talk than they are in listening to what you have to say. Moreover, because most people are more interested in themselves than anyone else, paying attention to them is seen as a sign you're an intelligent, likable person.

Want people to think you're fascinating? Be an astronaut, found a multibillion-dollar company, or, alternately, listen to them. In fact, after the initial thrill wears off, many people would prefer to spend time with a great listener who makes them feel important rather than the important person they're expected to orbit around.

Moreover, you'd be shocked at how much listening without judgment will open up communication channels with many of the people you care about. When people you love know that they can tell you anything and you will only want to help, it'll make them more willing to open up and deepen your relationship.

Some people are afraid to go that route because they translate "listening without judgment" to agreeing with whatever the person says. Obviously, you wouldn't do that. If someone is sleeping with the heavyweight champ's wife, having unprotected sex with prostitutes, or shooting heroin into their eyeball, you can't give them the thumbs-up. Of course, you also don't get the opportunity to gently steer them in the right direction if they know you're going to scream at them instead of listening to what they have to say, because they're not going to tell you.

Be the sort of person you can tell anything to. Not only will it make your friends happy and improve your relationships, but people will feed you a seven-course meal of intriguing stories and fascinating details.

19. If you have trouble telling people "no," the broken record technique comes in handy.

Do you ever find yourself caving in after being pressured by a pushy salesman? Do you find people at work or friends aren't listening to what you're saying? Are you talking to your kids but they're so excited that they're not hearing you?

If so, then you need to know about the broken record technique. Let me show you how this works:

Salesman: Listen, buying this extended warranty would be the smartest thing you've ever done. You do not want to put your investment at risk. You make a mistake like that and everything is out the window! So, should I put you down for the four-year warranty or the five-year warranty?

You: Thanks for the offer, but I don't want an extended warranty.

Salesman: Pretty much everyone who comes in here gets the extended warranty. In fact, we sort of thought you were going to get it. If we'd have known you weren't, I'm not sure we'd have given you such a good deal on the product.

You: Thanks for the offer, but I don't want an extended warranty.

Salesman: All right, all right, you drive a hard bargain, but I tell you what I'm going to do. We'll cut 20 percent off the cost, but if we do that, you do have to get a five-year warranty. I'll also need to get approval from my boss. I'll go ahead and go ask him . . .

You: Thanks for the offer, but I don't want an extended warranty.

Salesman: [Sigh] Okay, I'll have them bring it out front. I guess my mother was right when she told me I would never be any good at sales [begins openly weeping].

Some people don't like this technique because they think it's rude.

That's not so. Rude is refusing to take "no" for answer. Rude is ignoring what you say and trying to manipulate you into doing something else. Rude is treating what you're saying like it's not important.

To the contrary, the broken record technique allows you to answer rudeness or poor listening politely but firmly in order to get your point across.

It's also highly effective because when you're sticking to one point and won't get off of it, there's usually not much left to do other than to accept that your mind is made up. When you're hemming and hawing or making excuses, a salesman, a coworker, or a child has every reason to keep talking, but when you keep repeating "No thank you, I'm not interested" or "Put your toys away, brush your teeth, and go to bed," they know that's what you mean.

Learn this technique, love it, and add it to your repertoire. It's not something you have to use every day, but when you need it, wow, does it make life easier!

20. This is how to deal with the police.

I have a lead foot, and over the course of my lifetime I've probably been pulled over a dozen times. Once, when I was covering a clash between uncooperative protesters and hundreds of cops in riot gear, I even had a police officer point a gun at me.

The first thing you can learn from that is to not deliberately get in the middle of a protest where hundreds of cops are going to be clashing with agitated protesters.

Getting beyond that, you're going to be pulled over by the police at some point. When it happens, don't panic. Calmly grab your license and registration, stay in your seat, put both hands on the wheel where the officer can see them, and say "Yes, sir" and "No, sir" when you're talking to him.

Why should you be so polite to a police officer when he's giving you a ticket (!!!) and *you* help pay his salary with your taxes?

Because he doesn't know you from Adam, he views you as a potential threat, he has a gun, and he may very well have the discretion to increase or decrease what you're being charged with based solely on his mood. If there's going to be a big argument with a police officer, your lawyer should be the one having it in front of a courtroom full of people, not you by your lonesome on some deserted stretch of highway. You don't yell at the police, ignore their orders, or make any sudden movements. That may save you a beating or a night in jail at best and getting shot at worst. Besides, when you're polite to police officers, especially if you're a pretty woman who cries a little bit, a speeding ticket can easily turn into a "warning ticket" with a male officer.

Besides, unless you're really racking up the speeding tickets, you can almost always get out of them if you hire a lawyer. It stinks having to pay a lawyer plus an exorbitant court fee, but it beats having your insurance soar into the stratosphere.

But what if you're arrested for something more serious? What if you really did it? Then, don't be the dummy who tries to get out of trouble by making up some dumb story. Cops are naturally skeptical, and they're good at sniffing out BS. Instead, use the magic words, "I'd like to speak to a lawyer." Having a lawyer doing the talk for you may save your life or at least keep you from having to spend a great deal of it behind prison bars.

21. Right or wrong, good or bad, the more you achieve, the more criticism you'll receive.

Most people absolutely *love* the idea of getting famous. Having people recognize you everywhere you go, asking you for autographs, and treating you like you're special sounds amazing, right?

Except what few people realize is that the more people whose lives you impact, the more people there are going to be who hate your guts.

Oh, but I'll be nice! Doesn't matter. I'll work hard to make people like me! Doesn't matter. But I'm a good person! Doesn't matter.

Miguel de Cervantes wrote in *Don Quixote*, "Virtue is persecuted more by the wicked than it is loved by the good." In other words, if ninety-five people like you and five despise you, don't be surprised if you hear more barbed criticism from your five critics than you do love from your ninety-five fans.

You don't have to be a world-famous rock star to have this happen, either. In fact, the first time I was ever introduced to this concept was in high school. Our female class president was gorgeous, personable, and came across as a genuinely nice person. She always seemed to have a smile on her face, and she said "hello" to everyone from the star quarterback to the most unpopular kids in school. She sounds great, right?

So I was surprised when one of my female friends told me she couldn't stand her. I said, "She's one of the nicest persons I've ever met; so why don't you like her?" Her response? "No one can really be that nice. She's fake!"

As I got older, I got to see this kind of thing on a more personal level as my columns became more popular and my website took off. I have had every nasty thing you can imagine said about me, and every part of my body has been negatively critiqued in detail. After a while, you become so jaded, that kind of hate mail stops bothering you, but it wasn't just the attitude of strangers that changed. As my daily readership grew from twenty thousand people a day to five hundred thousand, yes, I did reach a lot of new people, but a number of acquaintances also turned unfriendly or into outright enemies as well.

If you don't think the same thing will happen to you if you start to get attention because you are really good at *anything*, then you're deluding yourself. If you get a promotion at work, then I can almost guarantee you that a certain percentage of people you were laughing it up with in the break room will start telling people you're a brownnoser or you got more credit than you deserved for some project.

The sad truth is this is part of being human. In fact, I guarantee you that 99 percent of the people reading this book have an irrational dislike for some famous person based on almost nothing. Maybe you think some singer from a boy band is too feminine or an actress is too trashy or you detest some politician over one out-of-context remark that you didn't bother to dig into to find out what he really meant. For all you know, these people are great human beings who regularly give large sums to orphanages because they want to help people, but you've trashed them all the same. So did I. So did your sister. So did the guy who fixed your car and the woman who checked you out at the grocery store. This is what people do.

The point of this isn't to stop you from becoming great at anything; it's to prepare you for a little piece of what comes next so you don't think "it must be me" when that kid you used to hang out with in high school randomly decides you're a jerk after you have a little success. Trust me, you'll make it just fine without him.

22. You must learn the art of ignoring.

When I was young and insecure, I felt like I had to respond to every challenge. "You're talking smack? Then I'm coming right back at you twice as hard!" That made me *feel* tough, but it wasn't true. After all, who's tougher: the guy who has to immediately respond to any challenge or the guy who is so sure of himself that he doesn't even feel the need to respond?

If someone tells a supermodel she's ugly, do you think she's getting in a twenty-minute back-and-forth fight over it or laughing, rolling her eyes, and moving on? If some guy tells a UFC champ that he can kick his ass, do you think he feels like he has to prove himself or is he going to laugh and think, "Seriously?"

As someone who writes about politics for a living, I have had every nasty thing you can imagine said about me. On a regular basis, I'm told that I'm stupid, fat, racist, fascist, ignorant, evil, and mean. Every body part I have has been negatively critiqued in detail. I get death threats. I get quasi-death threats (somebody should cut your throat). And you know what? I don't bother to respond to 99.9 percent of them because they're irrelevant. As the great Frederick Douglass once said, "A gentleman will not insult me, and no man not a gentleman can insult me." Unless someone starts handing out prizes for responding to random idiots on the Internet, it doesn't benefit me to engage with these people.

When you feel strong and secure as a person, you don't need to respond to every challenge. If some drunk guy in a bar starts talking trash, you walk away if you can. If your girlfriend is in a terrible mood and says something designed to get under your skin, you ignore it. When some twerp on the Internet tries to pick a fight, you ignore him.

Don't get me wrong: there is a time to put someone in his place. If that drunk guy at the bar backs you into a corner and puts his hands on you, beat him like he stole something. If your girlfriend starts regularly "getting into a mood" and treating you like garbage, then you need to let her know she's crossing a line and you aren't having it. If that twerp on the Internet is annoying, block him without hesitation.

Now some of you are reading this and thinking, "All that sounds great, but I don't want to be a doormat." If you're thinking that, you're getting this whole concept wrong. Nobody should allow himself to be abused, pushed around, or mistreated. However, if you don't end up in jail tonight because you had to "defend your honor" in some drunken bar brawl, are you going to be better or worse off tomorrow? If ignoring that one comment from your girlfriend spares both of you a big fight and leads to her apologizing later, wasn't that the right way to handle it? If ignoring that irritating comment on the Internet means you get to have a productive night instead of spending the next two hours going back and forth with someone you don't even know, wasn't that a better decision?

Learning when to ignore will change your life for the better or at least spare you a lot of fights with your significant other.

Chapter 4

NO REGRETS

23. Don't take naked pictures of yourself.

When I was in college, a guy I barely knew broke up with his model girlfriend after dating her for years and asked me out of the blue if I'd like to see a naked picture of her. Then there was the middle-aged mother who was naked on a webcam, trying to turn on a roommate of mine. He invited me in and asked if I'd like to watch. Another female friend of mine uploaded naked pictures of herself to a web server and a hacker downloaded them. Another female friend had an ex-boyfriend post her naked pictures on a public web forum. Then there's the other friend who had an ex-boyfriend send her a filthy pic that she took as a potential threat to take the other photos he had public.

On top of all that, I've had at least a half-dozen women send me naked pics over the years, and although nothing bad ever happened to them, *most of them* eventually reached out and asked me to delete the pictures. So, at a minimum, these women spent some time worrying about what would happen to those pics, and then they had to take my word that I deleted the pictures. Of course I did, but how can they *really* know that? They can't.

Even if you keep control of your pictures on your computer or your cell phone, it still doesn't mean they're safe. Hackers or maybe even curious friends who happen to be at your place while you're not there may somehow get control of your pics on the computer. Cell phones get lost all the time. Maybe the pictures are being saved on a "cloud" some-where—point being, as long as they exist, the possibility of their getting out into the world also exists.

Ladies, I'm sure you already have enough problems in your life with-out worrying about your parents, your boss, and your potential future husband getting to see you naked as the day you were born or, worse yet, playing out some kinky scenario involving peanut butter and a schoolgirl outfit with a guy you dumped three years ago because you caught him cheating on you.

Guys, let me make it even simpler for you: women don't want to see your penis. They really don't. That may sound unlikely to you because you're visual and enjoy seeing a woman naked, but women are wired dif-ferently. How differently?

Well, I once had a friend who told me she went to three or four differ-ent clubs that had male strippers. I asked her what she thought of all the chiseled men jumping around in front of her. She said, "It was funny." The word "gross" was also used—and you think a picture of your junk is going to get her revved up? At best, if she likes you, she'll roll her eyes, play it off, and then laugh about it later with her girlfriends. At worst, she's going to be disgusted with you even if she's polite enough not to say that it's "funny." Fellas, don't be *that guy*. Just don't.

24. Don't put anything on social media that you would be uncomfortable with the whole world seeing.

Human beings have this awful tendency to think that because they've gotten away with something once, twice, five times, ten times, that they'll keep getting away with it forever.

You want to know why couples who know better get pregnant after not wearing a condom? This is it. Do you scratch your head in puzzlement trying to figure out why someone who's gotten away with drunk driving keeps doing it until he hits someone else or gets in a wreck? This is it. Why does a woman put up a picture of another woman grabbing her boob on Facebook? Why does a guy have up a picture of himself about to pass out drunk? Because they get away with it. Their friends don't say anything or they laugh it off with a "You're so crazy!"

Then the girl's hunting for a job with a new employer or the guy has a date and the new employer or date does the most natural thing in the world these days. They check out the candidate online. What does a Google search pull up under your name? Do you have any pictures on Facebook that would make you look like a jackass? Are there tweets out there that someone who doesn't know you could misinterpret?

Do you want to be the guy who gets roughed up by a cop and has a prosecutor saying, "What do you expect, Your Honor? Here he is tweeting the lyrics to F*** tha Police." Do you want your mom to look at your Facebook page for the first time and see a "funny" image you put up about blowjobs? How about having a potential employer getting his introduction to you by reading a borderline racist comment you made on the Internet?

Don't be Cautionary Tale #5733 that everyone points to about the dangers of making dumb comments on social media. You have enough issues in the real world without creating more virtual problems for yourself.

25. It's best to avoid temptation.

I don't know what your weakness is.

Maybe it's food, alcohol, porn, smoking, gambling, heroin, or other people's wives. Maybe it's something else—but there is *something*.

You know what it is, and if you're being honest with yourself, you know exactly why you shouldn't be doing it.

Well, there's a reason why it's your weakness. Somewhere deep in the recesses of your brain, there's something going, "This makes me feel the way I need to feel!"

It's not simply a thought; it's a neurological pathway.

So, you may feel strong. You may feel prepared. You may feel like you have infinite willpower. You may feel like your weakness is no threat at all to you—and you may be right ninety-nine times out of one hundred.

However, that neurological pathway is still lying there, like a slumbering dragon. You have that one bad day; you slip that one time and everything can turn into an ocean of flame and claws.

Ever heard someone say "An object in motion stays in motion?" That's true—and not only for objects. You wake that dragon up and as often as not, he'll be pillaging the countryside for months. One cupcake can lead to a months-long binge. One drink can lead to another trip to a rehabilitation clinic. That one time cheating on your wife can lead to an affair that destroys your marriage.

Since that's the case, is ninety-nine times out of one hundred good enough?

Know how to make it one hundred times out of one hundred? Avoid your weakness altogether. If you're tempted to break your diet and go to Taco Bell, take a different route so you don't even see the store. If you're an alcoholic, don't go in the bar. If you're married and think you might cheat, don't allow yourself to be alone with an attractive woman who isn't your wife.

That doesn't make you weak or mean that you lack willpower; it makes you smart. Don't be the stupid guy who insists that you have infinite willpower the day before you go off the wagon or who cheats on your wife and ruins your marriage. Be the smart guy who avoided those temptations.

26. There are some things you shouldn't do because you might enjoy them too much.

The Bible is a book that's famous for encouraging people not to sin, but even the Good Book admits that sin can be pleasurable for a season. Furthermore, in our "If it feels good, do it" society, many people will tell you that you're foolish to deny yourself pleasure.

Unfortunately, this sort of thinking mistakes the happiness of the moment with joys of a lifetime.

There are some activities you shouldn't do because the short-term pleasure may keep you coming back even though the long-term price may be high.

Even if you've never taken crack or meth, it doesn't take a genius to tell you that the reason so many people try those drugs is that it will make them feel good. Let's say you're on vacation to Nevada where prostitution is legal. Is it okay to go see a prostitute? Even setting aside all moral concerns, ask yourself what happens if you have a great time. Then, are you going to be back home, where prostitution is illegal, trying to decide whether to risk breaking the law to get laid again? Does the idea of a one-night stand sound enticing? Imagine the feeling you have right after that one-night stand is consummated when you realize the condom broke and now you're having a conversation with a woman you literally met that night about what's going to happen if she gets pregnant. Incidentally, that happened to me once. I dodged the bullet, but you might not.

On another, personal note, I wish I'd never eaten cake, ice cream, a candy bar, or chocolate chip cookies because I don't eat any of those sugary garbage foods anymore, but I'm always going to know how good they taste and will have that temptation in the back of my head.

Again, I'm not talking about morality, trying to spoil your good time, or even telling you that if you try marijuana once or get drunk off your behind that you're going to be hooked. You didn't roll off the pumpkin truck yesterday, so you know better.

What I am telling you is that when you dabble in certain areas, you can't think only about tonight; you have to think about the potential long-term repercussions because every great journey or descent into the abyss starts with a single step. Watch where you're going because there are some things you can't unsee, unknow, or unfeel in life.

27. Avoid the big mistake!

At first glance, you're probably thinking, "Oh, thank you, super genius, for telling me not to make a huge, life-wrecking mistake! I had never thought of that before! Geez!"

Except, here's the thing: people do incredibly stupid things that have the potential to set them back for decades all the time and they keep getting away with it—until they don't.

They drive drunk, they go into a dangerous neighborhood to buy drugs, they shoplift, and it works out fine for them. Contrary to what you read in fairy tales, the good guy doesn't always get the princess and the bad guy doesn't always get what's coming to him . . . at first.

This is where people's perceptions get skewed. They wonder why evil people prosper. They wonder why the good get punished. They come to believe that they're bulletproof and all those consequences they've heard of are for other people.

Then they get a bad batch of drugs and have a heart attack, get caught cheating on their wives, or have sex without a condom and get pregnant. Sure, babies are a blessing, but it might not seem that way if you're seventeen and have to drop out of high school to take care of your kid, or the guy that knocked you up after a one-night stand gives you herpes and turns out to be an unbearable jerk who won't pay child support.

I'm all about positive thinking and doing what you can with what you have, where you are. However, you can still put yourself in a huge hole that you may have trouble digging out of for a long, long time. You get that job as a stripper, and five years later your fiancé hears about it and dumps you. You break the law, get caught, and twenty years later you still have trouble getting a job because you went to prison. You cheat on that one test you weren't prepared for, get kicked out of school, and never get your degree. You don't have any health insurance and a drunk with no money or car insurance rear-ends you. Next thing you know, you have $25,000 in medical bills trailing you around for decades.

There is a little bit of good news about all this. Most people know what to do; they just don't do what they know. You know you're supposed to wear a condom, you know you're supposed to buy health insurance, and you know you aren't supposed to be buying drugs from some shady, potentially violent thug.

Yes, there are a few people who are genuinely blindsided when they screw their lives up, but 95 percent of the time, the person who blows it *knew* they were doing something that had the potential to take a Jaws-size bite of their behinds. Take a hard look at your life right now and ask if you're doing something that could screw up your future. Then, cut it out! At least take some *reasonable* precautions. Don't bet your life that you're going to continue to luck out!

28. Don't stay in a bad situation because you are afraid of change.

Do you know the easiest thing to do when you have a problem in life?

Nothing.

Just keep doing what you're doing. You're overweight and out of shape? Keep eating too much and stay on the couch. You're in an awful relationship where you fight all the time; the sex is bad and you spend all your free time complaining about your boyfriend? Stay with him and hope it gets better. Is your job paying the bills, but you spend every day being miserable because you're burned out and hate your boss? Then hang in there and hope it improves. Somehow.

This is what most people do in life.

Change is uncomfortable, it's disconcerting, and it takes a lot of effort. Losing weight is anything but easy. Upgrading your boyfriend means enduring a possibly traumatic breakup, dealing with the emotional aftermath, and then going on what may turn out to be unpleasant dates. Getting that new job might require going on dozens of interviews or, if the job market is bad enough, moving to a new city.

It's easy to keep putting off a change over and over again until you realize you've let it go for months or even years. Worse yet, the longer you put off doing the right thing, the more difficult it often becomes. Let a problem with your health go, and your body can go much further downhill. The longer you put off making a change in a relationship, the easier it is to tell yourself that you have "too much invested" to make a change. When it comes to a job, if you're unhappy, you're probably not very good at what you're doing either, so it won't exactly be shocking if you end up getting fired.

You only have one life to live; how much of it do you want to waste mired in a bad situation waiting for a miracle that's probably never coming?

29. Avoid writing emails, letters, blog posts, or even having conversations with someone if you are upset with them.

One of the worst things anyone can do is blurt out every stupid thing that comes into his head when he gets angry.

You know what I'm talking about.

You're in a foul mood and someone you care about says something indelicate that you'd normally shrug off. Unfortunately, because you're mad, you lash out, and next thing you know, instead of having a nice, quiet night, you're experiencing World War III in your living room.

After seeing an idiotic comment online, you fire back, and next thing you know, you've wasted an hour, said a half dozen dumb things, and you're upset. Right about that time, you remember why people say you shouldn't get into fights with pigs—"because you get muddy and the pig enjoys it."

A friend is in a bad mood and says something rude that he'd normally not say; then you fire back; the two of you go back and forth and the whole thing turns into a big deal.

That last scenario once cost me one of my best friends. We started going back and forth about marriage. I told her if I were ever married, I'd have a prenuptial agreement. Because she had been divorced before and felt like she got a raw deal, she was apparently extremely sensitive about that and had some harsh things to say. I was particularly offended when she said no woman would ever marry me and hung up soon afterward. I had a trip out of town soon after and we barely talked that next week. When we did, I let her know I was still offended, and she made it clear she wasn't sorry. We didn't talk for months after that, and when I did try to open up the lines of communication, she refused to respond. Sadly, that was the end of our friendship.

Was the whole thing blown out of proportion? You bet. Was that a dumb thing to end a friendship over? Absolutely. Could I argue that she was more at fault because she also went a long time without talking to me and then wouldn't respond when I wrote her? Sure. None of that changes the fact that two good friends will probably never talk again because both of us got angry over something that was essentially irrelevant. It's not like the two of us were getting married to each other, so what difference did our views on the subject really make?

Whether you are a Christian or not, the Bible is right when it says, "A gentle answer turns away wrath, but a harsh word stirs up anger." Learn it, live it, and love it to save yourself a lot of problems over the long haul.

30. Be cautious about putting anything in an email that you wouldn't want to become public.

Strangely, many people treat online conversations like they're not quite real. They send out naked pictures and assume they'll never be seen by anyone other than the intended recipient, they put up pictures they'd *never* want a boss or relative to see, and they say things they'd never tell another person face-to-face.

People do this because they usually get away with it. Usually. Unfortunately, when they don't, the results can be devastating.

For example, when I was much younger, I had a job doing technical support. Much to my chagrin, one of the first calls I received was from a man who was upset because he found some dirty emails one of the people who worked there had been sending back and forth with his wife. I had no idea what to do with the call, and when I talked to my supervisor, he refused to take it. Eventually, I somehow managed to pawn the call off on a secretary. How that call eventually was resolved, I have no idea, but I'm pretty sure both that employee and that man's wife wished they hadn't been so careless about the emails they were sending.

Then there's the classic "I hit reply-all instead of just reply" mistake. You do not want to be telling some guy about all the dirty things you want to do to him and accidentally send it to half your office—and, yes, that does happen.

Of course, we also can't forget the people who make the terrible mistake of sending a threatening/racist/generally vile email from their work account. Next thing you know, the recipient is on the phone with their boss and is cleaning out their desk, wondering how they could have been so stupid.

Remember, when you put something in writing, if it comes back to haunt you—how you felt, the tone you were trying to get across, or what the other person said to you—it probably won't be treated as important; only the words you wrote will matter.

If you're writing about doing something illegal, think about how it would sound in front of a judge. If you are emailing another woman or man, think about what your wife or husband would say if they saw it. If the subject is your job, would your boss be okay with what you wrote?

As someone who works in politics, I assume *every* email I send may end up published somewhere. Incidentally, sometimes that assumption proves true. You may think that's not something you have to worry about, but in today's "everyone's a journalist" world, if you say something controversial, it may end up in front of an audience.

So, if you want to tell someone to go screw himself, tell people about what a jerk your boss is, or talk to your girl about all the dirty, filthy things you want to do to her, don't do it via email. Speak the words where there's no one recording it. That way, if they do ever betray you or run their mouth a little too much, there's nothing in writing showing what you said, and it's their word against yours. If you say something dumb, especially if you say something dumb, that can be the difference between getting a pass and having your life thrown into chaos for the foreseeable future.

31. Focus on the positive.

I hate to tell you this, but you're going to make a lot of mistakes in your life, and many painful things are going to happen to you. You're going to love people who don't love you; you're going to get dumped; you're going to be humiliated; friendships are going to end; and people you love are going to die. This happens to the poor and the rich, celebrities and the anonymous, the president and the guy who sweeps the White House floors.

So, when bad things happen that have a big emotional impact, what are you going to do about it? You can accept it and deal with the ramifications, or you can relive that misery over and over again. There are a lot of women who look like models walking around with a self-image that was formed by a bunch of little girls calling them "Tubby Tina" or "Crazy Carly" when they were twelve.

Does that help anything? If you have your heart broken, does reliving the moment she told you she never wanted to see you again make you feel better or worse? I can tell you from personal experience—it's the latter. Does it solve anything? No, she still doesn't want to talk to you. What's healthier, letting it go and trying to find a new girlfriend or spending months thinking about how painful it was for you? You already know the right answer.

Deaths are the same way. There are people who *never* get over the death of a loved one. That's almost disrespectful because it turns someone who loved you and wanted nothing but the best for you into a specter who's haunting your life and making you miserable. Holding on to that sort of grief longer than you should is almost a way of saying, "I loved you so much that I am going to continue to make myself miserable to show the depths of my devotion." This is not something that anyone who loves you would ever want you to do. If you love me when I die, share some of my writing, remember the good times, and go on with your life. Suffering because I'm gone doesn't honor my memory. Living a good life does.

There are people whose entire lives can end up being centered on traumatic events, and the reason that can happen is that they keep reliving it. What you focus on is what you move toward. If it's sad, miserable, and depressing, then you are moving toward sadness, misery, and depression. Wouldn't it make more sense to focus on where you want to go and what you want in life?

Controlling what you're thinking about isn't always easy. For example, you've probably heard someone say, "Try not to think of a pink elephant."

Of course, you can't help yourself and you think of a pink elephant. Do you know how you avoid thinking of a pink elephant in that situation? You actively force yourself to think of a purple elephant and you will be so busy thinking of the purple elephant, your brain won't have time to focus on the pink elephant. Do this with unpleasant thoughts. When your brain brings up an unpleasant situation, force yourself to think about something else. In other words, every time your brain starts into that same old, tired script, "I loved her so much and it didn't work out," break the pattern. "Yes, I did love her and I'm grateful for the time we had together. I can't wait to find someone even better." It won't feel natural at first, but it will work if you stick to it.

Negative thoughts are going to happen, but the more you dwell on them, the less time and energy you have to think about how to be happy, productive, and successful. Don't stay locked in an unhappy past when there's a future to be won.

32. Don't ever forget you're going to die someday.

When you're young, you feel like you have all the time in the world to achieve your dreams. Because of that, it's easy to kick the can down the road instead of going after what you want right now.

You stay in a job you don't like with no future because it's comfortable and safe. You stay at home watching movies and playing video games instead of going out and trying to find the girl of your dreams. You keep putting off having kids, going to Spain for the Running of the Bulls, training for a marathon, or learning to shoot because you have all the time in the world . . . until you don't.

Circumstances can change in a heartbeat. As you get older, your sperm count can unexpectedly drop and you find that kids are out. That marathon? That Running of the Bulls? You're one foot or knee injury away from never doing either of those things. It's also too late to learn how to get a gun and use it when three or four masked men break into your house and are headed up to the room where you and your family are cowering, defenseless.

Most people like to say that they have no regrets, but I'm not one of them because I wish I was married with kids. Unfortunately, in my twenties, I knew enough people who had been divorced that I told myself I wouldn't get married until I was thirty. About that time, I moved to a much smaller area than I realized and found my dating prospects were more limited than I anticipated. Worse yet, I learned that dating someone in their late thirties is a lot different than dating a person in their twenties. Anyone you date at thirty-five or older probably has a kid and a lot of mental scars from a previous marriage that didn't work out. It's no longer just a matter of "are you compatible," it's "is the trauma from their bad marriage going to ruin your relationship" and "do they have so much baggage that it makes you reluctant to move forward."

What it all comes down to is that time is not on your side, and if you spend your life waiting to get what you want, you may never get it. Don't be one of those people who puts off all their dreams until they retire someday only to find that they don't have the money, inclination, or wherewithal to get what they want out of life when the time comes. Figure out what you really want in life and start working toward it now instead of at some magical point in the future that may never happen.

Chapter 5

MONEY MATTERS

33. The keys to long-term finances are your house and your car.

One of the dumbest things I've ever heard a genuinely smart person say is that your car is a big part of your image. Maybe if you're Batman or Speed Racer that's true, but not so much for the rest of us. Ultimately, your car is nothing more than transportation. That's why billionaires like Mark Zuckerberg from Facebook and Steve Ballmer of Microsoft rather famously drive cars that cost less than $30,000.

Furthermore, let's assume you aren't a billionaire and a car is a big financial purchase for you. Over the course of a lifetime, your choice of cars can be the difference between getting to retire one day or spending your golden years working as a greeter at Walmart.

Currently, the average cost of a used car is $15,000, while the cost of a new car is roughly $31,000. Furthermore, the average person buys about ten cars in a lifetime. Given that the median income in the United States is a little more than $51,000, simply buying used instead of new is enough to save you three whole years' worth of income.

Then comes where you live. Once you get beyond the eating-ramen-noodles and grabbing-furniture-off-the-side-of-the-road-because-you-have-no-money stage of existence, housing is the area most likely to empty out your wallet. Show me people who're making decent money and still struggling to pay their bills (there are a lot of them), and nine times out of ten, it's because they have more house than they can handle. Instead of stretching to rent an apartment or pay the mortgage, most people would be much happier if they chose something they could easily afford.

Sure, it's nice to live in a big house with a beautiful view, but you know what's even nicer? Being able to sock away enough dough to pay your bills on time and not getting into screaming fights with your spouse because you're paying way too much every month for where you live. "Stuff" will never make you happy long term, but expensive stuff like cars and houses may make you miserable if you break the bank paying for them.

34. How do you decide whether to spend money?

I was amazed when I got my first credit card in college. Not only did it make me feel like an adult, but it felt like a huge lifestyle enhancer since I had so little money. Of course, it never occurred to me to ask why a credit card company would want to risk giving a credit card to an irresponsible eighteen-year-old kid who only worked in the summers and lived on a meager allowance from his parents during the school year.

After I used my credit card for brilliant purchases like party supplies and couldn't pay the money back, I learned why the credit card company did such a seemingly illogical thing. It *expected me* to make dumb purchases that I couldn't pay back, which would lead to my getting hit with huge penalties. I had to pay those penalties along with the money the company loaned me with interest. *A lot* of interest. So much interest that by the time my broke behind finally got it paid off, I paid off more in fees and interest than I had spent on goodies.

That was dumb.

Let me tell you what smart is: smart is setting aside money every month so you'll have enough to last you for a while if you lose your job or have a major car repair. Smart is setting up a budget and trying to stick to it. Smart is having the money to buy something, thinking you'd enjoy it, but *still* not spending the cash because you don't think it's worth that money.

True story: I know a guy who lived in a trailer and drove a fifteen-year old car for quite awhile even after he started making $100,000 *a month*. So, why didn't he move into a nicer house? Because he liked the one he was living in just fine and didn't feel like he needed more space. Why didn't he buy another car? Because the old one ran just fine. Besides, while there are benefits to having people know you're making boatloads of money, there are also huge downsides. People hit you up for money. They hint that they want you to pick up the check. Contractors and employees feel comfortable trying to get top dollar out of you. But if you're living in a trailer, driving a fifteen-year-old car, you can still do anything you want to do and go anywhere you want to go, but you don't have those problems. That's something to think about if you ever start making so much money that other people start getting upset that you're not paying even more in taxes.

In the interim, while you're waiting to get to that point, stop buying things for yourself because you "deserve them." You deserve what you can afford to pay for after earning the money. Nothing more, nothing less. Budget, prioritize, look for ways to get by on a shoestring, and always, always, always close up your wallet if you don't feel like you're getting your money's worth.

35. If you can, bargain.

If you're working with someone you can bargain with on a price, it seldom hurts to try. The exceptions may be someone of exceptional talent, someone you're going to work with on a regular basis, or someone whose help you're going to need in a timely manner.

Once, a political campaign wanted to hire me to do some consulting work. I asked *double* the amount I thought my services were worth, not because I thought I'd get it, but as a negotiating tactic. Well, guess what? No one batted an eye at that amount.

There's a lesson there and you should learn it.

When it's time to negotiate for a salary, it almost always pays to ask for significantly more than you want. Unless you go so far over what people think you're worth that they don't think there's a point in trying to work you down, it won't hurt you at all, and it may make you more money.

The same goes for when you're buying things. If you're not at a big chain store, make an offer and see if people will take it. If they don't, well, then you haven't lost anything.

I love to do this with gyms: "Yeah, I could sign up again, but the gym down the road is cheaper than you. You guys are more convenient, though. What if we did the same contract but made it for fourteen months instead of twelve?"

Here's how you do it. First, figure out your target. How much of a raise do you want to get? How much do you want to pay? What salary do you want? Once you get it in mind, confidently overshoot by a significant amount. Do you want a $10 raise? Ask for $20. Do you want to pay $100 for something at an estate sale? Offer $75. Do you want to make $40,000 a year? Ask for $45,000 or maybe even $50,000.

It's the job of the people you're negotiating with to work you down on your rate, and typically, they will do that. They'll counter your offer, and you respond by hesitantly agreeing to go down a bit. If they meet your offer there, great. If not, get down to the amount you really want to deal at and make a big play. "I tell you what. I didn't want to go this low, but if you make it $40,000 and throw in an extra week of vacation, we have a deal." Worst-case scenario, they're going to turn you down flat and you can get up, act like you're about to walk away, come back, and take the deal if you think it's worth it.

Refusing to do this is like taking money out of your wallet and leaving it on the table for no reason. Why would you waste your money like that?

36. In a business deal, make sure you have an ironclad contract.

Unless you're dealing with your parents or someone else whose life you'd stake on their word, you need a contract if you're engaged in a business deal.

It doesn't matter if a person is your friend, if she promises you a really good deal, or if she goes on and on about how honest she is; business is business. In fact, when someone expounds at length about her Christianity or how you can trust her, it should raise your hackles. Why? Because you don't need to take anyone's word for how honest she is if you can read it in the contract.

If you start engaging in business dealings with someone and there is no contract, you'd better either have some extremely powerful leverage or you should prepare to be screwed—and chances are, you will be screwed. Maybe you'll be screwed because she's inherently dishonest, or maybe she won't intend to screw you at first but will later because she can. Maybe she will really mean what she says, but then she'll get into a financial jam and tell herself that she "had no choice" other than to screw you. In life, you'll find that human beings can be remarkably flexible about what they consider "honest behavior" as long as they're the ones profiting from it.

Since that is the case, don't ever sign a contract that has clauses in it that you can't live with. There have been times when I've renegotiated a half dozen clauses on a contract. It doesn't matter if it's supposedly "standard" or if someone would "never use it." Contracts are supposed to be mutually beneficial, and it's better to walk away from a deal than sign on to one that has the potential to bite you in the butt down the line. The last position you ever want to be in is standing in front of a judge after you've been ripped off, telling him you might have signed the contract but you didn't ever think you'd have to stick to it.

37. Compound interest is your friend.

Saving even a relatively small percentage of your income each year, starting at eighteen, can leave you in much better shape by the time you're ready to retire.

If I looked back through my life and tried to identify the biggest quality of life changer, it wasn't later on when I started raking in the dough. Granted, that was nice, but the biggest difference maker for me was when I finally saved up enough money to cover my expenses for a couple of months. It gave me a genuine sense of security to know that if I lost my job, I'd still be able to pay my rent, or if my car broke down, I'd be able to pay to get it fixed. Surprise bills are an unhappy fact of life, and putting some money away makes them much more tolerable.

How do you do that when you don't have much money? I can tell you from experience it's tough, but there is a key to doing it. Set the money for your savings aside every month *first*, before you do anything else. If you get a check, take 10 percent and put it in your savings or investment account, and then live off of what's left. It will hurt for the first month or two, but after that, you'll adjust and won't even notice it. Furthermore, you will accumulate money faster than you might expect, especially if you consistently sock away "extra" money. What's extra money? Your parents give you money for Christmas; your grandmother dies and leaves you $5,000 in her will; you sell those old baseball cards you found in the attic for $500. Don't spend that money on a car radio or new shoes; sock it away. The same goes for raises at your job. Take half that money you get from a raise and put it into your savings. That way, you still feel like you're getting a raise, but your investment portfolio can keep growing.

Over time, because of the magic of compound interest, you would be shocked at how little money you need to set back to guarantee your financial future.

For example, do you want to be a millionaire without signing an NFL contract or becoming a pop star? Start putting $200 a month in an index fund at eighteen years of age, and keep doing it for the next fifty years. Over that period, you'll spend $130,000. Meanwhile, the stock market has historically gone up at roughly a 7 percent-per-year clip. Some years it's better than that, other years it's worse, but that gives you an idea of what to expect long term. If it continues to increase at that same rate and you reinvest your profits, you'll have a million dollars at sixty-eight years old. In the interim, you have the security of knowing you have a large nest egg in the bank if you get in a jam. So, who wants to be a millionaire?

38. For something you will use for a long time, spend a little more money and get something that is high quality.

When you don't have a lot of money, you are always tempted to spend as little as you can on any product. That's often a good impulse because when you don't have enough cash flow coming in, you don't want to waste any of it. However, there are times when it's not smart to buy the cheapest thing available.

For example, even though I had to pinch pennies for a long time, I always tried to get a high-quality computer, monitor, and desk chair. Why? Because I made my living writing and running a website. I spent a lot of time on a computer and I wanted one that ran fast and was easy to see. I also wanted to sit in a chair that didn't make my ass hurt.

If you want a more general example, think about your mattress. It's designed to last for a decade, and you're probably going to spend one third of your life during that period lying on it. Do you want the cheapest mattress you can find? I did that for a while. My parents still had the twin mattress I slept on for a decade as a kid. I used it at college. I was being smart and saving money, right? Except it wasn't a good mattress to begin with and, I kid you not, eventually the middle of it collapsed like a sinkhole. I can still remember curling my body like a question mark to stay on the edges. It was not a comfortable way to sleep, and after I ended up wrecking my back by acting like a contortionist, I gave in, bought a first-rate mattress, and started to get some decent sleep. Since then, I've never hesitated to buy a better mattress as opposed to the mattress that seems like the best deal.

Are you going to buy electronics? Don't buy old ones at some yard sale or flea market; pay the extra money and get products that work. If you run every week, get nice running shoes. If you go shooting regularly, get a decent gun. If you're on a construction site and handle rough material every day, get some first-rate work gloves.

You don't have to be the person who buys the best of everything. I have no qualms about buying used products, shopping at discount stores, or looking for the best bargain on a product. However, when it matters, you need to buy quality. The extra money you spend will be worth it when it makes your life easier.

39. Protect your downside.

One of the smartest pieces of advice I've ever heard is "Protect your downside, and the upside will take care of itself." This is a principle billionaires like Warren Buffett, and Richard Branson live by. Put another way, "Don't ever risk more than you're prepared to lose."

How does this work with finances?

Let's say you have a chance to get in on an investment that will pay you 50 percent on anything you invest this year, but you have a 20 percent chance of losing every dime you put into it. Meanwhile, every safe investment you can find only pays 3 percent per year. Do you invest your money in something that high risk and hope to make a killing this year? You do—if you can afford to lose the money. If you can't, you happily take the 3 percent.

If you're discussing the terms of a contract, you don't sign on the line that is dotted if there's a term you can't live with in there.

If you're gambling in Las Vegas for the fun of it, how much do you bet? Never more than you can afford to lose.

Do you want to be the test case for a lifesaving drug? If it's do or die, do, but if you can afford to wait a couple of months and let some other poor suckers try it first, that's protecting your downside.

If you want to go to a concert but the only person you can find to watch your baby is your irresponsible cousin who would probably forget your child existed for three hours if his girlfriend came over, do you go? No, because you can't risk your baby.

Some of you may not like hearing this, but if you have money, you don't get married unless your partner is willing to sign a prenuptial contract. I know that's not romantic and presupposes that things might not work out and you love her so much you want to be with her forever, but if you walk in on her straddling her old boyfriend on your bed a year into your marriage and it's over, can you live with her getting a big chunk of the money you've made in your lifetime? If the answer is, "Hell, no! Let her old boyfriend take care of her in that situation," you get the prenuptial contract.

Ladies, if things are getting hot and heavy with some guy and you decide to have sex with him and he whispers, "Come on, don't make me put on a condom. I'll pull out," what's the downside if he doesn't? It could be a baby with some guy you've been on three dates with. Furthermore, has he been tested for STDs? Aside from any moral concerns you have, protect your downside.

All of this probably makes sense to you, but all too often people get so excited when they have their eyes on the prize that they stop thinking practically. Tedious though it may be, if you don't protect your downside *every freaking time*, it can screw you. You can do the right thing one hundred times in a row, and that one time you throw caution to wind and bet everything on a single throw of the dice, it can come up snake eyes and end you. Don't be that cautionary tale. Protect your downside.

40. If it sounds too good to be true, it probably is.

When a financial deal looks too good to be true, three pertinent questions to ask are: how much risk is there, how sure are you that the deal is legit, and how is it that such a fantastic deal came to you?

Most young Americans are living off their relatives or working starter jobs, so they don't have much money to invest. Still, at some point if you're smart or lucky, you will have two nickels to rub together and you'll start thinking about investing your money.

While investment advice is beyond the intended scope of this book, it's worth reminding you of what billionaire Warren Buffett has said, "Lesson: Rule No. 1: Never lose money. Rule No. 2: Never forget Rule No. 1."

That rule is even more important for you than it is for Warren Buffett because he has so much money that he could afford to blow a few million dollars as kindling for his fire. Since you probably can't say the same, it's important that you don't lose what you have.

So, before you invest, it's crucial to ask yourself how much risk is involved. Although the stock market has consistently grown at about 7 percent per year over the long term, there's no absolute guarantee that will continue. Moreover, there can be huge year-to-year fluctuations, and individual stocks sometimes lose all their value. Sixteen months after Enron hit an all-time high of over $90 a share, the company was bankrupt.

Sometimes deals that are too good to be true will fall into your lap. People get scammed every day on the Internet by "Nigerian princes" offering to make them rich if they'll help move millions into the country. You'll just need to send a few thousand dollars for advance fees.

Of course, there's the question you always have to ask yourself when you're faced with a situation like that: If this is such a good deal, why aren't these people bringing it to some well-heeled rich guy instead of me? Maybe there's an answer for that question, but if you aren't absolutely certain of what it is, then don't risk your money on it.

Chapter 6

ADULTING

41. Chart it.

You want to lift more weight? Write down your exercises, reps, and sets at the gym and make sure you're going up. Want to lose weight? Write down what you eat every day so you can see how many calories you're consuming. Want to find places you can cut money out of your budget? Write down what you're spending every day. You might be surprised at what you find.

I certainly was. At one point I started drinking a delicious, lemonade-flavored vitamin water. I loved it and started drinking more and more of this tasty beverage! Then, I started writing down how many of those bottles of lemonade I was drinking. It turned out to be six per day at a dollar a pop. So, yes, I was spending $180 a month on *lemonade*. Not kidding. Before you laugh at me, consider that there are many people who spend even more on coffee, cigarettes, and going out to eat for lunch at work. That's not necessarily a bad thing if you have the money to spend, but if you are hurting for cash, you might be shocked at how much of your money is being spent on I-can-take-it-or-leave-it items every month.

That happens all the time.

It works this way because we human beings are good at misleading ourselves. We excuse ourselves when we screw up. We block out the times we fall short. We treat trends like one-time events and one-time events like trends. Next thing you know, we don't understand how our performance can be so poor when we "almost always" do a good job. Meanwhile, "almost always" may have been less than half of the last month. This goes on and on until we're forced to confront reality. That can be through a crushing failure . . . or through charting. Trust me; you'll prefer the charting.

42. Keep a clean house.

Here are the keys to keeping a reasonably clean house. Don't leave any dishes in the sink overnight; every time you have a full load of clothes, wash 'em; take out the trash every time the can is full. You do those things, wipe up your messes, and vacuum when the floor gets filthy, and you'll keep things reasonably neat.

I used to *hate, hate, hate* to clean and I was *very* sloppy. I mean, I wasn't quite "hoarder" level sloppy, but it was pretty bad. I'd eat and leave the dishes in my room. I had clean and dirty clothes piles. When I'd get done with things, I'd leave them where they fell. I had roommates get mad at me over it; an apartment complex sent me a letter of concern after a guy spraying the complex saw my place; friends came over and I wouldn't let them in the house because it was so nasty. This was not something to be proud of.

Then, about the time it occurred to me that it would be nice to bring friends or, better yet, women to my apartment, I got some advice that changed everything for me.

It centered on three parts of the house.

When you cook food, you put the dishes in the sink and you don't leave any dishes in the sink overnight.

Your clothes go in a laundry hamper, and after they're washed and dried, you hang them up.

You put trash in a trash can, and when it's full, you take it out.

Now, will doing only these things keep your house clean enough to make your anal-retentive, germ-phobic mother happy? No, but it will keep your place clean enough to allow it to pass for a presentable bachelor pad. You'll still need to vacuum occasionally, scour the stove, dust, clean the baseboards, scrub the bathroom, etc., but if you don't do those things for a few weeks, your place will still be relatively clean and you won't endure anyone saying something like, "Oh my God, what is growing in your sink?"

In other words, think of these things as the bare minimum you have to do, even if you hate to clean, and you'll never have to go to the doctor with a stomach bug, like I once did and have him ask (this really happened), "Have you been drinking from any outdoor streams?"

43. When you move, sell, throw away, and give away as much as possible.

Like a lot of young Americans, I changed apartments a lot. I'd become annoyed with a roommate, find a place that was closer to a job, or a place that was cheaper, then off I'd go! Yet, what did I find when I moved? I would be moving boxes of stuff that I hadn't looked at in years from the closet in my old place to the closet in my new place. (P.S. As a side note, you find out a lot about who your real friends are when you move. Anybody who's willing to show up and help you move a couch with just some pizza and beer as compensation is probably someone you'll want to try to keep in your life.)

My *parents* were even worse. They moved from a large house to a smaller place at the beach. Even though they sold a lot of stuff when they left, they had furniture sitting in the yard at their new place! They found spots for some of it, but more than a few pieces rotted, became covered with mold, and had to be thrown away.

In life, you accumulate loads of crap—things you thought you'd use but never did, things that were nice at one point but need repair, and boxes of junk you never sort through. Then, what happens? Your house gets more and more cluttered. You run out of space and you move things from closet to closet. You know you should throw this junk away, but you don't want to take the time to sort through it or, worse yet, you remember how much it cost you, not what it's worth right now.

People seem to put a high value on "things," even things they would have trouble selling for $5 at a yard sale, but they often don't put the proper value on having a clean, uncluttered, spacious environment. The value of a thing to you should not be derived from what you paid for it; it should come from how useful it is to you right now. If it's not valuable, get rid of it. Sell it if you can; throw it away if you can't. It'll make a bigger positive impact on your life than you realize.

44. Dogs are fantastic animals, but they are much more expensive and time consuming than you'd think.

One day, my roommate brought home a dog. His parents didn't want it anymore, but his sister loved it, so he agreed to keep it. I quickly became attached to the dog, but my roommate wasn't as fond of him for understandable reasons. We were told the dog was house trained, but it turned out that was with a doggie door. He was crapping and peeing all over our apartment. Worse yet, he had separation anxiety so bad that he chewed a hole in the couch. After a few weeks of that, my roommate didn't want him anymore, so I agreed to take responsibility for him. Even though I didn't have a lot of money, I figured it couldn't be all that expensive, right?

Wrong.

My dog was finicky about what he ate, so that dry dog food? I had to abandon it for much more expensive wet dog food. His treats? Not so cheap either. A toy he didn't tear to pieces in five minutes? $10. Then there were the other bills. Grooming? $60. Shots? $50. The dog's knee popped out of joint, which was a common flaw of his breed—$150.

Then, toward the end of his life the bills *really* stacked up when the poor little fella got cancer in his nose. There were constant vet visits, none of which were cheap. Eventually, the vet wanted me to spend thousands of dollars for one scan of his nose to confirm a diagnosis he was 99 percent sure was correct. Since the only option after that would have been a surgery that cost thousands of dollars and still provided a poor quality of life for my buddy, I decided to pass. Of course, then I had to pay to put him down.

The cost was much bigger than I ever anticipated, and I also didn't know he'd be hostile and angry with houseguests. He even bit a friend of mine who stayed with me for a few days. Her pet name for him was "demon doggy." He'd run away from the house if he slipped out the door; he sometimes got in fights with other dogs; he once even made me take him outside to pee in the middle of a Category 2 hurricane, which didn't seem to perturb him in the least, despite the howling winds that made me wonder if a tree limb was going to fall off and mash in our skulls.

Last but not least, when you're sitting down with your trusting but scared little buddy hiding between your legs, about to give the order to a veterinarian holding a shot that will end his life, you think really hard about what he'd want. My dog had the heart of a lion and I don't know that he would have wanted to be put out of his misery. I just knew he couldn't breathe properly, get comfortable, or sleep for more than an hour or two per night and that it was only going to get worse. It's still not easy to be the one who makes that life and death decision.

I'm not telling you this to discourage you from getting a dog because Patton was my pal and I loved him to death. I am glad I had him in my life and, as I write this, my dog Jackson is curled up at my feet. That being said, you need to know what you're getting into if you get a dog. Take it from a guy who had a dog eat a hole in the side of his couch: If you're not a pet owner, expect it to be more expensive, time consuming, and difficult than you expect.

45. Lefty is loosey. Righty is tighty.

It's never fun when the tire on your car goes flat, and it was more problematic than usual in my case. I had managed to get the car into a convenience store parking lot and had a spare, but there was a big problem. The mechanic who put on my tires had apparently used a pneumatic torque wrench that had made the lug nuts on my car so tight that none of them would move an inch. I was putting so much pressure on my handheld wrench that it started to bend, but absolutely nothing was happening. Worse yet, because there was no movement, I wasn't sure which way to even turn the wrench. Was I making the lug nuts *even tighter*? I didn't know.

Just as I was about to give up and call a tow truck, two Hispanic guys were walking by and asked if I needed any help. I said "yes" and let them take a crack at it. They had one big advantage that I didn't: They definitively knew which way to turn the wrench because of a simple saying: "Lefty loosey, righty tighty." The lug nuts were so tight that all three of us had to take cracks at them, but we got the job done. After we were finished, I gave them $50 that they seemed to be embarrassed to take, but eventually did after I reminded them that a tow truck would have cost more than that. It was well worth it, not just because I got my tire changed, but because I learned something valuable.

Are you trying to change the lug nuts on your car? Are you trying to loosen a screw? Are you trying to open a stuck jar? Whatever the case may be, remember lefty loosey, righty tighty. If that seems simple, it's because it is simple, but those four little words will make life a lot easier when you take things apart or put them back together.

46. It's worth your time to take a typing class.

I have many strengths as a human being, but coordination is not one of them.

True story: When I was young, my parents were called to a special school conference. They thought the school was going to tell them I was some kind of super genius because, you know, that's what parents think of their children. They were surprised when they were told that I had a learning disability. My hand-eye coordination level was extremely poor. Do you remember those old-school panty hose eggs? It took me a couple of minutes to put one of those together.

So, as you might imagine, typing class was quite the challenge for me in high school. Even though I busted my butt, I was lucky to make it through with a C.

However, now, in my forties, it turns out that the most valuable class I took in high school was . . . you guessed it, history. No, just kidding. It was typing.

Why? Because despite the fact that I was never very good at typing, I can still crank out thirty words a minute, which is extremely useful for someone who writes for a living. Even if you don't write for a living, you still probably use a computer, and if you use a computer, you probably do a lot of typing. Being able to type instead of hunting and pecking will make everything faster for you. If you even semiregularly use a computer, this will save you thousands of hours over the course of your lifetime. So whether it's in high school, college, or online, take a typing class. Until we get advanced enough for you to think words onto the screen, this is a skill you need to master.

47. Don't underestimate the impact of sleep on the quality of your life.

Take it from someone who spent more than a year of his life struggling to get more than four to five hours sleep per night because of a workload that could kill a horse: you need sleep.

It impacts your mood, your health, and your attitude.

How often have you woken up feeling like a sack of monkey crap, staggered into work late, and then spent the next few hours struggling to stay awake because you didn't get enough sleep? How many times have you eaten garbage you'd normally never touch because you're so tired you're about to keel over? Have you ever begged off of doing something fun with your friends because you needed zzzzzs so bad you wouldn't enjoy it?

Lack of sleep is a real problem for people, particularly in the modern era. You want to know what it takes to get a good night's sleep?

- It's worth spending a little more money than you'd like to get a good mattress. While you're at it, get a decent pillow to lie on and one for in between your knees.
- Don't watch TV on your bed. Don't work on your bed. Ideally, don't do anything in your bed except go to sleep.
- Control your environment. Avoid stimulants right before bed. Make your room cool and *dark*. Use blackout curtains if necessary. Turn off or cover up any digital glow that lights up your room. Turn off the TV, computer speakers, and anything else that may wake you up.
- Even though I don't have any problems with sleeping, according to various sleep trackers I use, I'm "restless" seven to nine times per night. Do you know what you do when you wake up in the middle of the night like that? You close your eyes and go back to sleep. But what if you have to pee? Keep one eye open, do your business, and get right back into bed and go to sleep.

- This one is key: turn off your cell phone. I once had a woman sleeping over at my house who often complained that she could never get enough sleep. It was easy to see why. Even though it was late at night, every two to three minutes, her phone would alert her that she had received a text, an email, or a response on social media. Several times, she reached over and turned on her cell phone to look at whatever message she had and kept fiddling with it for another three or four minutes. After this kept happening over a period of twenty minutes or so, I was ready to take her phone and toss it out the window. No wonder she said she had trouble sleeping! I am to sleeping what Picasso was to paintings, but even I wouldn't be able to fall asleep with all the nonstop cell phone action she had going.

Before you take sleeping pills, warm baths, or *cold showers* (this really wakes you up, then causes you to crash hard) or start spending a lot of money on trackers designed to monitor your sleep, do the basics and your sleep problems may fade away before you know it.

48. Cars do require maintenance to function properly.

My first car was a piece of crap that broke down frequently as it got older. Granted, it wasn't the nicest car in the world to begin with, but I didn't get regular oil changes or tune-ups and I had a horrible tendency to hold off on taking the car to the mechanic even when I knew it had some minor problem. Something would be squeaking; the car would run poorly; it would overheat, and I'd still hesitate. I told myself that I didn't have the money. Of course, I *really* didn't have the money when my car finally overheated so badly that it did almost a thousand dollars' worth of damage to the engine and left me stranded on the side of the road.

Of course, things are just things. They're not as valuable as human lives, especially *your own*. I knew my tires weren't in the best shape, but because I didn't pay much attention, I didn't realize they had gotten so bad that the cables were wearing through on one of the tires. That turned out to be quite relevant when I was driving back on a country road in the middle of a pouring rainstorm and there was quite a bit of standing water on the road. I hit that water and hydroplaned for what seemed like an eternity. I kept turning the wheel to keep from going off the road. When the tires got traction again, the car spun wildly out of control, flipped over, and I landed upside down and backward in a ditch. In those three or four heartbeats when the car was out of control, time somehow slowed down, and to this day I remember thinking, "So this is how I'm going to die." The force of the crash was so violent that it literally broke the seat and I ended up in the backseat with my head through a stained glass window I had been taking back with me. I was amazed that I was alive, but I hesitated to turn my head and look back because my dog had been in the passenger side front seat and I figured he was dead. I figured wrong. A small, shaken dog walked up to me, and both of us were all right. Sure, the car was totaled, I had a hairline fracture in one of my fingers, and I needed stitches for my head, but that was practically miraculous given the situation.

So, how about you? Do you need to blow out your engine or have a near-death experience to learn to take care of your car? Do you need to end up stuck on the side of the road somewhere or upside down in a ditch like I was to learn this? I did. Learn from my mistakes.

49. If you are cutting something, make sure you are cutting away from your body, not toward it.

Throughout your life, you will be working with various sharp objects— knives, scissors, chainsaws, buzz saws, you name it. Because you will use sharp objects semiregularly to do everything from chopping food to opening packages to cutting tags off clothes, it's easy to forget that you're using potentially dangerous tools.

Unfortunately, if you're careless about using those tools, you may end up with the nickname "Stumpy." Sure, you can be careless with a knife or a chainsaw ninety-nine times and you'll be perfectly fine, but that hundredth time you can end up with a chunk of yourself on the floor. Even if it's not that bad, do you really want stitches? You have to waste time at the hospital, it's painful, and you can end up with a scar. Depending on how deep the cut is, you can end up with a scar *and* permanent damage to the tendons or nerves as well.

"So, what are you telling us? Be careful with knives? Thanks, genius! None of us ever thought of that!"

No, I'm not just telling you to be careful with knives, I am telling you that when you are cutting something, make sure the blade is moving *away* from every part of your body. What you don't want to do is have the blade moving *toward* any part of your body, like your hand. This is a small distinction that can determine whether you get to finish your life with ten fingers or not; it's definitely something you should always have in the back of your mind when you're working with a sharp object.

50. Here's how and when to tip.

First of all, almost everyone knows that they should tip a waiter or waitress, but not everyone does it. However, if you can't afford to tip a waitress the proper amount, then you can't afford to eat dinner. If the waitress gives good service, 15 percent is the standard tip you should leave. That goes up to 18 percent if it's a large group.

But what if you don't get good service? What if the food is late? What if you're parched because your waitress never fills your glass? What if your waiter is a jerk? You will hear varying opinions on this, but if you don't get good service, then your waitress doesn't deserve a good tip. If the service is flat-out terrible, I don't tip at all because that's the proper way to let wait-ers and waitresses know they're not doing a good job. You don't *ever* yell at anyone handling your food unless you enjoy having gross foreign substances inserted into your dinner. You don't write snarky notes on the receipt that give them the opportunity to make you appear to be the bad guy. Just leave them the tip they deserve and everything else will take care of itself.

Now here's where it can get confusing: Waiters and waitresses aren't the only people who get tips.

For cabbies? You want to hit 15 percent of the fare. The pizza guy or anyone else who delivers food to you? 15 percent. Your hairstylist or bar-ber? 15 percent. The lady who does your manicure or pedicure? 15 per-cent. A massage therapist? 15 percent.

Things get a little cheaper at hotels. If you're talking about a door-man who brings your bag up to your room, a hotel employee who brings something to you, a washroom attendant, coatroom attendant, or some-one who parks your car, that's $1 to $2.

When you get beyond that, things can get a little sketchy. I've had a girl at Subway ask for a tip after she made my sandwich. She looked so fantastic in the short shorts she was wearing, I gave it to her. The people who groomed my dog? They asked for a tip. Once, when I was young and worked for a rental car company, I helped a customer with his bags and, even though I didn't expect a tip, I felt like a million bucks when he gave me $20.

At the end of the day, you are seldom going to feel bad about being a generous tipper, but you may be embarrassed if you don't tip someone what they deserve. Think about that before you pull out your wallet and leave a tip.

51. Prepare in case it all goes wrong.

Most people tend to think of "preppers" who spend an inordinate amount of time and money preparing for a lifestyle-altering disaster as a little off-kilter. Of course, if there was a zombie outbreak tomorrow, where would everyone go? To the house of any prepper they could find because those people are equipped to survive and you're not . . . but you should be.

I'm not saying you should build a bomb shelter in your backyard or start living off the grid next week, but if a hurricane or a tornado struck and you were cut off from electricity, the supermarket, and help for a week, would you make it? Do you have enough canned food, water, working flashlights, and emergency supplies to last a week, and a gun so that even if things get crazy, you can hold on to your goodies? Take it from someone who has taken his dog out to pee in a Category 2 hurricane, you need to be able to take care of yourself for a few days because there may not be anyone showing up to rescue you.

Also, as you will see noted elsewhere in this book, it's wise to save up enough money to support yourself for six months even if you have no other income. Not only does that give you a little protection if you lose your job or are temporarily disabled for some reason, it'll give you some peace of mind because sudden bills won't leave you in debt or scrambling to figure out how to pay them.

Some people go way beyond that. For example, the Mormon Church counsels its members to store up a year's worth of food. That comes in handy not just if there's an emergency but as a guarantee that even if you lose your job, you and your family will still be able eat.

Of course, the real question is, "How far do you go with this?" Because, after all, if you want to *really* be prepared for anything, you'll probably need some land out in the woods with its own water supply, a bomb shelter, massive amounts of supplies, guns to guard it all, and a set of survival skills that could take you years to learn.

This creates a dilemma for most people because if they pour all the resources into prepping that they need to be ready for the apocalypse, it'll cut into their resources so much that they may end up in the poorhouse. It's a little like getting fire insurance for your home that's so expensive you can't pay your mortgage. You don't have to go to that extreme, but you do need to be ready to take care of yourself for at least a little while if it all goes south tomorrow.

Chapter 7

HEALTH

52. Take care of your body for the first forty years of your life, and it'll take care of you for the next forty years.

When you're young, you feel nearly invincible, and no wonder. You stay up all night and you still have the energy to work all day. You get the same flu your father gets and he's down for a week while you're down for a day. You gain fifteen pounds and after dieting for a few weeks, it melts right off of you.

Unfortunately, this does not continue throughout your life. As you get older, typically it takes longer for injuries to heal. You have less energy, you lose muscle mass, and your metabolism slows down.

Worse yet, injuries accumulate. Even getting out of alignment and declining to deal with it can have consequences. The cumulative damage you do to your body starts to add up. If your back hurts regularly when you're younger and you have a bit of a funny walk, go to a chiropractor and get your frame fixed. Work on that while you're young because if you ignore those problems year after year, you may end up with a much worse injury when you're older. That semiregular twinge in your back may turn into something that can lay you up for days at a time at sixty. You have a little hitch in your walk? That may turn into hip surgery at sixty-five. A single careless mistake in the gym doing squats or deadlifts can leave you with an injury you'll have the rest of your life. Personally, I feel a weird pain in my shoulder in certain positions because once I got sloppy with my form doing assisted pull-ups. That's it. One mistake and it's with you forever.

Smoking, drugs, heavy drinking, being overweight—all these things take a toll on your body. A lifetime of smoking will often make a woman's face look like a catcher's mitt in her late forties. Drinking too much over the long haul can hose your liver. Depending on what illegal drug you're taking, your brain, your heart, or who knows what else in your body may be affected—and that's if you survive at all. Not everybody does. Being overweight can do damage to almost every part of your body—your feet, your knees, your heart, stretch marks. You don't want surgery to put in a new plastic kneecap in your seventies.

Until some mad scientist perfects brain transplants one day, you only have one body. Be careful because you will have to live with any big mistakes you make with it for the rest of your life.

53. If you think a doctor is wrong, don't hesitate to ask for a second opinion.

Take it from someone who has had not one, not two, but three close family members die after doctors made questionable calls: Do not take a doctor's word for it when your health is on the line. Some of them are terrible at their jobs, complacent, lazy, and careless. Even if they're smart, know what they're doing, and mean well, it doesn't mean they know what's best for you.

Let me give you a personal example.

In my late twenties, I had a potentially life-threatening blood clot develop in my right leg. After the initial successful treatment, my doctor didn't seem to have any answers for me. He didn't know what caused the blood clot. Furthermore, for whatever reason, my body did not react well to the blood thinner he had me on. One week my blood would get so thin I'd be at risk of bleeding to death if I were seriously wounded, and then after a slight adjustment, you couldn't tell that I was on anything. Meanwhile, the tests never stopped. Every week I had to get my blood tested. Then I'd talk to my doctor and he'd change my prescription. He gave me test after test after test, none of which ever seemed to be conclusive. Many months later, I finally realized his dilemma. If he told me to get off the blood thinner and I had another blood clot, he could be blamed. On the other hand, the blood thinner wasn't safe for me either because we could never get it stabilized in my blood. So, he was just killing time by giving me ever more useless tests and hoping some solution would reveal itself.

Eventually it did because I made an executive decision to get off the blood thinner. I certainly didn't want to be on those drugs for the rest of my life, and as it turned out, it was a good call. More than fifteen years later, I've never had another blood clot.

So, am I saying that you should ignore your doctor and do whatever you think is best?

Absolutely not. But if a doctor is going to cut into you, give you a dangerous treatment, or generally suggest any sort of potentially life-altering advice, you need a second opinion from another doctor. Talk to your doctor, take lots of notes, and then either go in to see another doctor or find one online. Once you're talking to them, see if their advice matches up.

Keep in mind that it may not. The second doctor may suggest another potential avenue of treatment or may have a less extreme solution you can pursue. When you're dealing with your health, don't take somebody's word for it simply because she's wearing a white coat unless it's an emergency situation and you have no other choice. In a worst-case scenario, that second opinion may save you a surgery or a painful treatment. If the second doctor agrees with your first doctor, then you should have a little more peace of mind.

54. Take care of your physical frame.

If you are fat, you know you need to lose weight. If you smoke or do drugs, you know you need to stop. If you never exercise, you know you need to get active. Most of these issues have been drilled into people to such an extent that there's no point in even discussing them.

However, there's a crucial element of long-term health that's rarely discussed until it causes a serious problem. That's your physical frame—your hips, your knees, your back, your feet, and the rest of your body.

Your body is a marvel of engineering because if a part of it stops working correctly, the rest of it will compensate. For example, if your hips are too tight, your quadriceps will take up the slack and you'll still be able to walk around just fine. If your head slumps forward, you won't get off balance and fall over like a domino. If your back or knee is sore, in most cases you won't be immobilized—you'll still be able to limp around like your grandpa.

The problem with this is that your frame is designed to last a lifetime, but *only* if it's in alignment. When you're young and your body is at its peak, you may barely notice if things are off-kilter. When you turn forty and you've had the same problems for twenty years, those minor annoyances can start becoming crippling issues that impact your quality of life. Your back going out can leave you disabled for days. Your knees may be shot so badly that you can barely walk. The pain and instability in your hips may cause you to fall.

Most people who are in that position don't get there because of a motorcycle wreck or a car ride; they get there because of decades of neglect of their own bodies.

If you don't want to be in that position, you need to start taking steps to protect it right now. At a minimum, start stretching every day. Right as you get up is a great time to do it. If you want to take it to the next level, try yoga or Pilates. If something goes wrong, get to a chiropractor. If the chiropractor can't fix you up after a few visits, head to a physical therapist who can do active release therapy, acupuncture, or dry needling. There are a lot of things you can try, but the worst thing you can do when something is wrong with the way you move is nothing.

Don't be the guy getting a metal knee at sixty or the woman who needs someone to hold her arm to get up the steps. As the old saying goes, *Listen to your body when it whispers and you won't have to hear it when it screams.*

55. Test yourself.

We human beings are so good at self-delusion that we can be unaware of things about ourselves that anyone who spent twenty minutes in a room with us could easily see.

Furthermore, because your friends and family don't want to hurt your feelings, they're typically going to be uncomfortable giving you open and honest feedback.

So, what do you do? You test yourself. There are an almost infinite variety of tests out there, and as someone who loves to experiment, I've tried a lot of them over the years. Here are the most useful ones:

The Myers Briggs: This test breaks people into sixteen different personality types that are freakishly descriptive. You'll find this test gives you an accurate picture of your personality along with your strengths and weaknesses. If you want to know yourself, this is where you start. (P.S. I'm an ENTJ.)

The 5 Love Languages Test: Many people don't realize it, but there are many different ways that people like to show and receive affection. There are words of affirmation, touch, quality time, receiving gifts, and acts of service. If you're like me and you prefer words of affirmation and touch while your partner shows how much she cares by picking up your laundry and making the bed, your relationship probably isn't going to last unless you understand what's happening. The 5 Love Languages test will enable you to do that and teach you something important about yourself during the process.

The Helen Fisher Personality Test: You can think of this one as sort of a hybrid of the Myers Briggs and 5 Love Languages tests. It's a bit like the Myers Briggs in that it tells you a lot about your personality, although there aren't as many variations. Furthermore, once you know your own personality type, the test gives you an idea of the other personality types you're likely to find attractive. In my experience, this test holds up pretty well.

There are some physical tests I'd recommend as well.

DEXA Scan: This is the gold standard for measuring body fat percentage. Not only is it extremely accurate, you're even told the breakdown of muscle to fat in different parts of your body. If a DEXA scan isn't available in your area or is cost prohibitive, a BOD POD scan is an alternative you may want to pursue. Although the DEXA scan is better in my experience, the numbers have turned out to be close.

A Functional Movement Screen: This is a test you'd typically get from a sports chiropractor. The FMS identifies weak spots in your movement patterns that may cause problems down the line. Once you identify those issues, you can start doing stretching and exercising to improve the way you move.

A Resting Metabolic Rate Test: This test will tell you how many calories you burn per day at rest. In other words, if you laid in bed all day long and didn't move, this will let you know the amount of calories you could eat without gaining weight. This is enormously useful because it gives you a solid starting point on how many calories you need per day to gain, lose, or maintain your weight.

As Socrates said, "The unexamined life is not worth living." It's time for you to use these tests to start examining your life.

56. Pornography is physiologically bad for you.

If prostitution is the world's oldest profession, then the second oldest is the guy who was paid to draw prostitutes at work with their customers. Granted, the porn was probably drawn on cave walls or carved into wood back then, but you can be sure that sex sold even back in the Stone Age.

However, today, because of the technology we have, pornography is only a click away on the Internet, and there's an ocean of it for you to swim in. It doesn't matter whether you have a foot fetish, are sexually attracted to people in animal costumes, or want to read some erotic fan fiction featuring your favorite movie characters, you can find it on the Internet in massive quantities.

Of course, it would be easy to give you a moral case against pornography, but if that dissuaded people, no one would look at pornography in the first place. Besides, you're an adult, and you're going to do what you want to do in the privacy of your own home.

That being said, have you ever considered the physiological effects of consuming porn on a regular basis? Biologically, you're driven toward sex, and if you're getting that need fulfilled at your computer every day, you're going to feel much less driven to get a girlfriend. Worse yet, when you do find a woman you want to be with, you may find that you're desensitized by all the pornography. Even if you get to the point where you have a beautiful naked woman in front of you, pornography may make you feel like she doesn't live up to the perfectly stylized scenarios you've seen on the screen. Additionally, masturbating is training your brain to get aroused through a method other than normal sexual contact. Because of that, many men who regularly watch pornography have trouble performing or even getting an erection.

Worse yet, think about what you're doing when you watch porn. Chemically, you're getting a huge hit of dopamine every time you masturbate. Because you have a virtually unlimited number of women and situations in front of you via porn, it can prove to be even more addictive than sex with a real partner. Because of this, it's easy to become like a rat in a lab, hitting that button to get your dopamine release over and over. For that reason, many pornography addicts feel an emotional deadness because, like any drug, the more of it you take, the more of it you need to get an effect. Suddenly, little things that got you excited or made you feel something don't produce any kind of sensation at all. This can lead to depression.

Pornography is a little like alcohol. There are plenty of people who drink and don't suffer any negative consequences. Unfortunately, other people can't control themselves around alcohol, and they end up doing everything from drinking and driving to destroying their liver. If you're consuming pornography on a regular basis and any of this seems familiar to you, then you need to make a change for your own sexual and emotional well-being. It may not be the easiest thing you've ever done, but it can make a huge difference in your quality of life.

Chapter 8

CAREER

57. There's no shame in taking an honest job.

During my lifetime, I've done a lot of crummy jobs. I worked the fry bin at Burger King, stocked shelves, slaved away in a group home, laid sod, sold Amway, worked for a temp agency, and took pictures at Walmart. Not only have I worked for minimum wage, I've worked for *free* as the equivalent of an intern at times. I can't say that I particularly enjoyed any of those jobs, but I'm not ashamed of working any of those places. Additionally, I'm happy that I don't have to do any of those jobs anymore, but if I were strapped for cash and couldn't find a better job, I'd work any of those jobs again.

Not everybody looks at it that way. Some people think they're too good for a certain job. Other people feel like if they've progressed a certain way up the ladder, they shouldn't have to go backward. There are even people who look down on someone who takes what they think of as a menial job.

My father worked his way up from the worst job in his company, punching holes manually in carpet, to vice president of that same corporation, and he was right when he said, "There's no shame in any honest job." Now, is there shame in living off your fellow man or being unable to take care of yourself? You bet. But a person who's willing to work and pay their own way can at least take pride in that even if they can't take pride in anything else.

So, don't ever, ever let anyone tell you that you should be ashamed of your job. It doesn't matter if your name is on your uniform, you're wearing a funny hat, or you're standing in front of a store twirling a sign in your hand; if it pays your bills, there's honor in it. It'll also give *you* something to talk about one day when you're doing well and people want proof that you're not just a rich jerk who was born with a silver spoon in your mouth.

58. Getting fired or laid off isn't the end of the world; sometimes it's a blessing.

Three of my lousy jobs are particularly noteworthy because I was fired from each of them. Well, I was technically laid off from my job doing tech support, but that one may have been the unkindest cut of all.

I had been there for years doing tech support in part because it didn't matter what I did when I wasn't on the phones. That meant I had a little bit of extra time to work on my website during the day. Of course, I didn't work on the website because I was fantastic at what I did. I was the guy who was given the screaming, irrational customers with unfixable problems when no one else could handle them.

Then one day the whole staff was brought in offsite for a meeting.

That was a bad sign.

Then a corporate VP walked up front and said, "The good news is that your jobs could have been sent to Canada . . ."

That was also a bad sign. A really bad sign.

As it turned out, another company was brought in to manage the staffing. We had the option of losing almost all our vacation and sick days, taking a pay cut, and continuing to work at the same desks, or unemployment.

Since I had been planning to quit and go full time on my website in a few months once I saved up enough money, I took option B and never regretted it.

That was typical of all the jobs I was fired from. I didn't particularly like any of those jobs, I had no future in any of them, and although it was tough making ends meet, ultimately I was better off for leaving.

Losing a job can be *devastating*. You feel rejected and sometimes even betrayed. Suddenly you don't know how you're going to pay your bills. Where is your next job going to be? Will it be worse? Better? More money? Less? Your whole life is uncertainty . . . and then it starts to get better.

You might have to suck it up, cut back, and scramble, but you'll make ends meet. You may not know what your next job will be, but if you put your best foot forward and look for one, more often than not you'll find something *better* than what you had. In fact, being fired is often a *good thing* because human beings have a tendency to become complacent.

Before you know it, you're halfheartedly working a crappy job, going with the flow, and trying to make it through the day. Then when you're forced to make a change, it's like you wake up for the first time in years. It makes you reexamine what you're doing for a living, how you're spending money, and what you're doing with your life.

Is it fun? No. But neither is getting a shot when you're sick. Look at losing a job like that. It's your opportunity to start healing your life instead of continuing to cough, wheeze, and sniffle through it with a lousy job you probably didn't even like in the first place.

59. Start looking for a new job *before* you quit your old job.

In my early twenties, I went through a lot of lousy jobs with low pay, bad hours, and annoying bosses. When you're in that situation, the frustration level builds.

For example, I hated being an assistant manager at Burger King. The employees were unreliable; some of the other members of management were stealing; my feet were killing me. Then there were the shifts. There were weeks when I worked a breakfast shift one day, a midday shift the next, and a late shift the day after that. On top of all that, there were hours of paperwork and cleaning that had to be done every night after a shift was over, and if you were short staffed, then too bad because management had to get it done.

I got to a point where I *hated* everything about that job. I hated eating the food on my thirty-minute lunch break, the employee who took twice as long as everyone else to make a Whopper, and the degrading managers' meetings where you'd be ordered to watch training videos again to make sure you knew how to make a chicken sandwich.

I had little time off to look for another job, made even less per hour than the regular employees if I divided my mediocre salary by the sixty-plus hours a week that I worked, and the pain from being on my feet twelve hours a day in work shoes didn't ever seem to go away.

Eventually, as I prepared to go into another weekend shift, I couldn't take it anymore. I picked up the phone, called in, and quit on the spot with no notice.

It felt *phenomenal*.

Unfortunately, as someone who was living paycheck-to-paycheck, I couldn't *afford* to do that. Suddenly, I was put in a position where I had to immediately try to get temp work if I wanted to pay my rent at the end of the month. As to job options, I couldn't afford to be picky because I had bills due. Moreover, quitting without notice made it harder to find a new job because Burger King sure wasn't going to give me a good reference after that.

That was an error I repeated several times until I got a little older and more responsible. Learn from my mistake.

Once you start becoming discontented with your job, start sending out resumes and move on when you have something bigger and better. Keep your options open. It may keep you from having your phone turned off because you can't pay the bill or taking a job as crummy as the one you're leaving because you have to keep the money rolling in somehow.

Show a little patience, a little foresight, and put in your two weeks' notice after you find another job. You won't ever be sorry.

60. Look for something you love doing so much that you'd do it for free, and find a way to make it into a career.

You're probably going to spend one-third of your waking hours as an adult working; shouldn't you be doing something you love? Do you want to be on year eleven of taking orders from a boss you don't like who's telling you to do a job you hate while you spend every free second getting yourself revved up for the weekend? Whoop-de-doo, you get two days off, and then it's back to keeping your soul from fleeing your body in response to the torment you're going through at work.

I have been there, folks—burned out, taking sick days because I couldn't bear to show up and do my lousy job, looking for anything to distract me because I hated my job so much. Sadly, many of the people reading this book will spend their whole careers in jobs like that because it's better than being homeless.

However, I have an alternate concept: Find something you love to do, and find a way to make that into a career. That may mean running your own business. It may mean going back to school to study something after you thought you were done. It may mean working a full-time job you don't like while you work part time somewhere else to gain experience at something you love.

I did it. As I mentioned, I took that full-time job doing tech support, in part because I was able to work on my website when I wasn't on a call. I spent four years working forty hours a week at my job, working another thirty to forty hours on my website, getting four to five hours sleep per night, and then doing it again. After four years, I was able to go full time when my website was pulling roughly 12,000–15,000 people a day. I didn't make much money back then, but I loved every second of it. Today, I still love every second of it, and my website pulls fifteen million people a month. I get up when I want to get up, go to bed when I want to go to bed, don't take orders from anyone, and love what I do.

You can have that in your life, too, if you want it badly enough and are willing to be patient. You just have to be creative about it and have enough confidence in yourself to disrupt your life a bit and take a risk. It's worth it to have a fulfilling career that inspires you to get out of bed in the morning instead of one that makes you pull the covers over your head because you don't want to go to work. If you're going to spend forty hours a week on something for forty years of your life, shouldn't you be doing something you enjoy at least a little bit?

61. Don't take any job that only pays commission unless you're an expert salesman.

Once, I had a friend who was *desperate* to move across the country. She was smart, talented, and charming but had very little cash. So, to make the move work, she needed to have a job waiting for her when she arrived in her new city. After an exhausting search, she found one. It was a commission-only sales job. I tried to warn her that she was unlikely to make enough money to live on that job, but unfortunately she didn't listen. Instead, she moved, started her new job, and two weeks in, she hadn't made a dime and quit. That started a long, unpleasant period for her in that city that got so bad, I ended up buying two weeks' worth of food and having it shipped to her house after she admitted she hadn't eaten in over a week.

Of course, some of you may be thinking, "I get a commission-only job, then I don't make enough money to buy food, and next thing you know, I've lost a lot of weight. That's the best diet ever!"

Before you start that diet, let me tell you about a roommate I once had. He was a fairly talented salesman and he had a commission-only job selling the large signs in front of businesses. In case you didn't know, those signs are expensive, and because it was commission only, he received a fairly large commission check every time he sold one. In fact, he was so good at it that he would work six months of the year, make a ton of money, and then he'd take the next six months off. Sounds like a good gig, right?

So, is every commission-only job a rip-off? No. In fact, some of the best sales jobs are commission only because they draw in the best salesmen. On the other hand, many of the worst sales jobs are also commission only because they're selling third-rate, difficult-to-sell products, and they would never be able to pay a talented salesman to take the job.

The key thing to keep in mind is that it takes a particular set of skills to be good at sales: charisma, the ability to close a sale, and the willingness to keep working even though you're getting no after no. If you have those skills already, you probably can tell the difference between a great job and a job you wouldn't touch with a ten-foot pole. If you don't have any sales skills and someone is willing to hire you for a commission-only job, you should question how good a job it is in the first place and, given that sales isn't easy under the best of circumstances for most people, prepare for a long, dry period until you can go all *Glengarry Glen Ross* on it.

62. Most businesses will see you as disposable.

When my father was growing up, there was a simple formula for financial success. You got a job with a good company, worked your way up through the ranks, and then retired one day with a gold watch and a pension. In his case, he worked his way up from manually punching holes in carpet to vice president. If you're not inclined to work for yourself, this potentially sounds like a pretty good deal, right?

The problem is that the mindset that created those jobs no longer exists on either side of the equation. Corporations will fire you for doing a bad job, but they'll also fire you if they can open a plant in India that allows them to hire people who do what you do for $3 an hour. They'll fire you if they can replace you with a machine. They'll fire you if they can hire another firm to bring in workers that are cheaper than you. They'll fire you because of corporate restructuring because they don't think you are making them enough money or because you've been around for too long and they can hire a younger worker or a foreign worker to do your job on the cheap. Workers are like tennis shoes to employers, and the moment the soles get a little worn or they can get a nicer, newer pair, you're in the garbage. Workers have responded to this mentality by walking their tennis shoes right out the door the first time they find a better opportunity.

You have to adjust to the world as it is, not as it used to be. What that means is that you need to evaluate your job. How are your pay and benefits? Do you enjoy what you do? Is there potential to move up, and if so, are you willing to do what it takes to do it? Have you already been promoted and realized there's nowhere else to go? Is the company making money or is it slowly falling to pieces? If you decide where you're working isn't the place for you long term, then you need to start looking around.

People tend to get comfortable in their jobs, but never forget it's a fluid environment, and any stability you think you have can disappear in a heartbeat. A lost business deal, a new boss, a change in plan by the company's owners, and everything can become different. Don't be the guy who spends way too long at a go-nowhere job and ends up bitter and broken years later after he's fired.

63. If you don't feel like you're being treated fairly as a consumer, don't hesitate to ask for a manager.

Supposedly "the customer is always right," but you wouldn't know that from the way some businesses treat you. When you get in that situation, it's sometimes tempting to scream at whoever is telling you "no." Sometimes I engage in that impulse myself with telemarketers who keep calling me early in the morning after I've already told them to put me on their no-call list. However, while it's emotionally satisfying to yell at peons, it often doesn't accomplish much. Jenny the checkout girl probably isn't going to have the authority to make you happy. Furthermore, it's not like she came up with the stupid rules that are driving you up a wall. So, if she didn't create the problem and doesn't have the ability to fix it, it's probably a waste of time to yell at her.

So, what do you do in that situation? You ask for a manager. Do you know who managers typically are at most places? They're people who used to work on the front lines but were good at dealing with people who are pissed off. So they were promoted and given more authority. This is who you want to talk to about your problem.

It's always nice to set it up by telling the front-line employees that you're "really angry and that you need to speak with a manager." You don't have to scream at them to get that across either. They will pass on the fact that you're angry to a manager who will immediately think, "Oh, geez, I just wanted to have a nice lunch and now I'm going to get yelled at for the next twenty minutes. Why did I ever take this stupid job in the first place?" When he arrives, if you have to yell, yell at him because he's used to it. Usually? I don't even bother to yell, although I do like to give little hints that I'm seething just to make a manager more likely to cater to me. (Maybe I can go back to my nice lunch *without* getting yelled at!)

Does this work? Usually, yes. What do you do if it doesn't? You can let it go or, as I sometimes like to do, you can keep working your way up the food chain to see if you can find someone willing to do the right thing.

Once, I had some terrible problems with an Internet hosting company that had an excellent reputation for customer service. For months my website went down and ran slowly, and the people who worked there were reluctant to help with it. When they did "help," it often wasn't useful. Once, they knocked my entire website down and it cost me a thousand bucks to undo the damage. I talked to manager after manager and got nowhere. Eventually, I had to move to a different company, and when I did, I wrote an article describing the misery they had created for me with their poor service. That article received quite a bit of traffic, and next thing you know, one of the company vice presidents wrote to me. He looked into my case, concluded that it had some validity to it, and gave me a few thousand dollars of my money back to make up for how bad their service had been.

There's a lesson there. If a company is treating you poorly, keep asking for the next manager up the chain until they refuse to let you talk to someone or you get what you want. More often than not, it'll work, and as an added bonus, you won't have to feel bad later because you yelled at some kid who just started his first job and got stuck defending a stupid store policy.

Chapter 9

SUCCESS

64. You beat 50 percent of the people by just showing up, another 40 percent by working hard, and the last 10 percent is a dogfight.

I once had a roommate who wanted to be a professional singer. After hearing him sing around the house, I didn't think he was all that good, but then again, I don't think Justin Bieber is all that good either and look how his singing career is going.

Anyway, I asked my roommate if he had a demo tape. He said "no." I asked him if he was in a band. He said "no." Well then, I asked, how was he ever going to be a singer? He said that he was waiting for a talent scout to discover him, presumably either at his day job, in our living room, or at the bar since that's where he spent most of his time.

As you may have guessed, this is not how the real world works.

Most of the time, the people who succeed are the ones who show up, work hard, and keep trying new things until they finally have some success.

That may mean changing jobs. It may mean changing states. It may mean working for free. It may mean working two jobs. It may be months or even *years* of not getting enough sleep because you need a day job while you try to turn your hobby into a career. It may mean watching people who aren't in your league move ahead of you for a little while because of connections or dumb luck.

Guess what? I've had *all* those things happen to me.

I had to put in years of brutal work to get to the point where I could work for myself and almost a *decade* more before what I was doing took off.

Is it worth it?

Well, I get up when I want to get up, go to bed when I want to go to bed, and I go on vacation when I want to go on vacation. I don't have a boss, nobody gets to tell me what to do, and if someone pushes me too far, I have the freedom to tell them to kiss my behind; I sometimes exercise that freedom.

I'm pretty happy with that, so for me, yes, it was all worth it.

Of course, I'm living my dream. Your dream may be different. Maybe you want to work your way up through the corporate ranks or become an indispensable well-paid employee where you work. Heck, maybe you want to make enough in the first half of every year to take the second half off and surf. Who knows?

The philosophy doesn't change. Show up, work hard, and keep pushing yourself to improve until you're where you want to be. Winning the lottery may sound easier, but that's a pipe dream, while this is a formula that will work if you give it enough time.

65. You're going to have to prove yourself.

True story: When I started as a blogger, I worked at my job eight hours a day, worked on my blog another eight hours, got four to five hours' sleep a night, and made almost nothing. After a couple of years, when I still had only a few thousand readers and was making almost nothing, a relative who regularly read my work said it was good but that I'd be better off quitting and spending the eight hours a day working as a bag boy.

Objectively, that was true. Back then, I would have made a lot more as a bag boy. On the other hand, I loved writing, felt like I was making progress, and believed I could make a career out of it. A few years later, I was running my own website for a living. Last month my website *Right Wing News* did twenty-two million visits. Let's just say, at this point, I'm doing a lot better than I could bagging groceries.

So, how did my relative get it so wrong when she knew me so well?

Easy.

The fact that she knew me so well made it *less likely* that she could see my potential because it's human nature to expect to see what you've already been seeing. Are you fat? Don't expect everyone to believe you when you say you're going to lose weight. Have you ever run a business? Then don't be shocked if the people around you doubt you can do it. Ninety-nine percent of people will believe you have what it takes five minutes after you prove it. Don't be upset about that because, like the saying goes, "Who cares if people believe in you? It's not their job to believe in you."

It's easy to believe Bill Gates can make another million dollars and Tiger Woods can win a golf tournament because they've proven themselves. If you haven't, then you must be disciplined, work hard, and show everyone that you're not all talk. Then, after you make it, all the same people who didn't believe you could make it will be telling you they always knew you'd do it, and you'll be struggling to remember when they ever said anything remotely like that. Be gracious when it happens because we both know you've done the same thing to someone else in your life.

66. Most happy and successful people persistently and consistently work hard, work smart, and do the right thing.

Rarely is success an accident, but when it is, rarely does it last.

Most people who are successful earned it. They worked their way up the ladder of a corporation, they put in seventy-hour weeks building their own business, they did without until they had what they wanted.

The same goes for failures.

Anybody can be poor, but if you stay poor in a country like America, it's your own fault.

Losers love to blame everybody else for their failures. They *had to* quit school. "Everybody" has sex without a condom; they were just "unlucky" and got pregnant. "Anybody" would have broken the law in that situation; they just got caught. "Everybody" goes deep into debt to buy an expensive new car and house. "Anyone" would use drugs if their friends were doing it too!

This is all happy BS loser talk.

It takes years for most people to claw their way up the ladder, and one serious mistake can ruin all of it.

This doesn't apply only to finances either.

If you want to run a marathon, bench three hundred pounds, woo a woman, or learn to play a guitar, it's going to take time, study, and consistent effort to make it happen. The people who are good at *anything* have usually put in crazy amounts of time and effort. Why should success be any different for you?

The good news is you're in charge of whether you're a success or a failure in life. Of course, for some people, the bad news is that they're in charge of whether they're a success or failure in life because they habitually screw up their own lives and point the finger elsewhere.

If that description hits a little too close to home, then do something about it! Stop being that person and become the guy who's willing to come early, stay late, and go above and beyond. You can have your dreams, but you must earn them!

67. Ironically, successful people tend to fail a lot more and ask more questions than unsuccessful people.

Sometimes we get so caught up in appearing smart that we become afraid to ask the question that will actually make us smart. It doesn't matter what the subject is or how much natural aptitude you have at it—there are going to be things you don't understand. If you don't ask questions, those gaps in your knowledge will keep you from ever reaching your true potential. In other words, the fear of looking dumb by asking a question will keep you dumb. Don't be the dumb guy who doesn't ask questions; be the person who asks questions until you know the subject inside and out.

Similarly, if you want to be successful at anything in life, you're going to fail an awful lot. As a matter of fact, you're going to fail a lot more than the *unsuccessful* people. That's because unsuccessful people fail a few times and quit, while the best fail and keep going.

I've certainly failed a lot in my life.

After one year of working forty hours a week on my website, I had one thousand readers. After two years, I had three thousand readers. I ended up going full time on my website earlier than I planned because I was laid off from my job. I was unable to get on with a speaking agency. I started an all-video website, a quote website, and a website dedicated to creating Facebook pictures that all failed. I reached out to another business owner with an idea for a joint venture, and he implemented my idea without giving me any role in it. I partnered up with someone on a graphics website. It failed. I partnered with someone else to create a link website. He re-created the website with a different name to cut me out of the partnership. People I mentored turned their backs on me when they no longer needed my help. There were people I helped, even though I received nothing of value in return, who smeared me publicly for not doing enough for them. I could go on and on with this, but the end result is a website that has over fifteen million people a month reading it.

Once you get past a few exceptions who are either lucky or are born into wealthy and privileged families, that's what it takes to succeed. Life knocks you down; you get up. It knocks you down, you get up. It knocks you down, you get up. Then one day it swings, you slip the punch, and you rain holy hell down on it until it lies there whimpering in submission long enough for you to finally get what you want . . . for a little while anyway.

Accept the challenge, take the beating life is going to dish out, and keep going until you get what you want. You're going to spend your life doing *something*; you might as well pay the price to get what you want.

68. Pick the brains of people who know more than you do.

There's a lot to be said for reading, watching videos, and formulating your own strategies, but you're going to get the best information about what you want to do from people who are already doing it.

You want a job at a company? Ask someone who already works there the best way to get hired on. You want to play music for a living? Ask a professional musician what to do. You want to be a professional writer, athlete, or even a successful politician? Ask the people who've already done it for advice.

They have the contacts and they also know the ins and outs you don't get from books. They may have been at the point you're at in your career, and because of that, they can tell you exactly what you should be doing right now. As the great Thomas Sowell has said, "Experience trumps brilliance." These people have already figured out how to jump the hurdles you're going to run into one day. Real brilliance is taking advantage of their experience so you don't have to go through the same thing.

These people are also able to tell you which public advice you're reading is real and which is phony. Take it from someone who owns a 3.3-million-like Facebook page—most of the advice on handling social media out there is pure garbage. Even most of the supposed "experts" don't have the slightest idea what they're talking about. I know that because I've done what some of those teachers have never done but are teaching others to do. It's like that with people who are good at anything.

I've had the opportunity to interview a lot of the most successful people in my field, and often, before I get started, I ask those people for advice. Furthermore, there have been a couple of fairly big-name people who I've reached out to and asked for a "mentoring session." Both of them said "Yes."

Why would busy, successful people agree to something like that? Because it's flattering to be asked to share the secrets of your success with someone who admires what you've done. I've had acquaintances ask the same of me, and I've always said "Yes." (That being said, I can't mentor everyone reading this book or I won't have time to do anything else, so I'm begging off on this one.)

Don't be shy about this. Ask, ask, ask, and it will get you so far ahead of the game!

69. If you want something, ask for it.

I used to love the saying, "If you build a better mousetrap, the world will beat a path to your door." It sounds great, right?

The only problem is that, as it turns out, it's not even remotely true. Worse yet, it encourages people to passively wait for someone else to give them a break. Most people who do that will grow old waiting for someone to come along and recognize their genius. There are scientists smarter than Einstein, women more beautiful than Marilyn Monroe, and computer geeks much smarter than Bill Gates who never went anywhere. Why?

Because when you want something, you've got to be willing to ask for it.

I am currently the most-read columnist on *Townhall*, which is one of the biggest conservative outlets. So, how did I get to that point? An acquaintance offered me a chance to do a single column at a different conservative outlet called *Human Events*. Not only did I do it, but I asked him if I could do a weekly column if my performance was up to par. I did well and suddenly I had a regular column. Then, the time came when I wanted to move to a bigger outlet, so I found out who ran *Townhall* online, noted the success I had at *Human Events*, and asked him to give me a shot as a writer. He did. The rest is history.

Did you know I'm overweight? It's true, but did you also know I managed to get Chris and Heidi Powell of *Extreme Weight Loss* fame to help me out? How did I ever get the help of two TV stars who are better than anyone else at helping people lose weight? I wrote them, asked for it, and they said "yes."

My best friend is amazing at this. If she checks into a hotel and there's something wrong with her room, she'll end up with a discount on her bill or an upgrade every time. I've seen her on the phone with an airline, talking them into cutting her a deal on no-refund tickets. Once, when I was driving into Myrtle Beach late on Thanksgiving, she thought it was appalling that I wasn't going to be eating with my family, so she swung into action. Next thing you know, she was telling me where to go because she had asked a family she knew to give me some traditional Thanksgiving food to take home.

Is there a girl you really want to date? Well, have you ever asked her out? Is there a company you really want to work for but it didn't hire you after you put in your application? Well, have you thought about finding some employees of the company, approaching them, and asking for advice on how to get hired there? Is there a party you want to go to but you weren't invited? Did you ask any of your friends if they were invited, and if so, can they get you in?

What's the worst that's going to happen? Somebody will tell you "no." So what if they do? It doesn't mean your life is wrecked, it doesn't mean they think less of you, and it doesn't mean you're going to be stopped from doing what you want to do. That's the beauty of asking. If one person tells you "no," you go to the next person and ask.

This works unless you ask every woman on the street corner to have sex with you, in which case you'll get slapped a lot. Also, you don't want to ask any police officers whether they pulled you over because they saw you mooning them. Be responsible, but ask and then ask again, and keep looking for ways to ask until you get what you want.

70. When it comes to life, your attitude should be, "If I didn't earn it, I don't deserve it."

It's fascinating how many people think the world owes them a living, presumably because they're so wonderful that the rest of us couldn't get by without them. In case anyone is worried about that, if the world kept on spinning without Einstein, Martin Luther King, Winston Churchill, and Jesus, it will make it fine without you. That can be depressing or liberating, depending on how you look at it.

Speaking for myself and, for that matter, most people, I deeply care about what happens to my friends, my family, and myself. Beyond that, I wish people well, but their personal problems are not my personal problems.

Many people aren't willing to admit that and they'll talk a big game about how important it is for someone (not them) to do something about a problem or for the government to take money from people (not them) to fix a problem. Most of the time, these are just people trying to steal a little virtue on the cheap.

On the other hand, if you are one of the people who really wants to personally help others, you have to help yourself first or you won't have anything to help others with. You need money to give them money. You need skills that can be of use to others. Even if you're just doing grunt work in a soup kitchen, you at least need to have free time available to make a difference.

Those are the sort of options you have when you learn to take care of yourself and make your own way in the world. The problem far too many people have is trouble telling the difference between "wanting" and "deserving" something.

So, people buy something they can't afford because they've worked hard and they "deserve it." They think they deserve a promotion, not because they're the best person in the office, but because they're the senior person in the office. Some people even convince themselves that they deserve things because they're a good person.

It almost seems cruel to tell people that if you haven't earned it, you don't deserve it, but telling people the truth to help them succeed in life is never cruelty.

You want to *deserve* that swanky $300 purse? Start setting money aside in a savings account until you have enough to pay for it. You want to *deserve* that promotion? Come earlier, stay later, have a good attitude, and outperform your competition. Make your boss *afraid* to pass you over because you're one of his best people and he can't afford to have you leave. Do you think you deserve to have a charming, stable, intelligent model girlfriend who loves sex and taking care of you because you're a good person who would be nice to her? Well, if you did somehow manage to get a date with a woman like that, would you be the type of man she was looking for as well, or do her needs not matter? Are you supposed to be able to land the feminine ideal just because you're a good guy, or do you need to bring anything else to the table? Well, to paraphrase author David Wong, there are plenty of other good guys in her life, and unlike you, some of them can play a guitar. What do you have going on in your life that genuinely makes you worth as much to her as she is to you? That's what "deserving it" is all about.

This is a difficult lesson for a lot of people to learn simply because they don't want to accept it, so they're always fantasizing about shortcuts. There's a reason the lottery is so popular, and people have always loved the idea of Aladdin's lamp. Everybody has wants, but it's hard to save money, suffer, and put in countless hours paying the price to achieve those wants. When you stop lying to yourself about what you deserve, accept that you are going to be alive for a long time, and may as well spend that time paying the price to get what you want, your life will change for the better.

71. Here's how to become a success at anything.

It doesn't matter whether you're talking about checkers, knitting, baseball, cooking, boxing, or farming, there is one simple key to become successful at it. It's taking all the money in your wallet, putting it in an envelope, and sending it to me . . . wait, that's not right. I mean, it can be if you like that idea . . . OK, OK, actually the simple key to becoming successful at anything is finding something you love to do and immersing yourself in it.

Why does it have to be something you love? Because if you don't love it, you're not going to be willing to spend hour after hour working on it.

Show me a guy who is six foot nine with great speed, a fantastic vertical leap, and tremendous athleticism who hates basketball and loves golf, and I'd bet he's much more likely to become a great golfer than a professional basketball player.

Why? Because the best people at *everything* immerse themselves in it. They learn every aspect of it backward and forward; they ask a thousand questions, read a hundred books, and work so long and hard at it that other people think they're obsessed. How do you do that if you don't love what you're doing?

Sure, some people will punch a clock every day for forty years and do their work for a paycheck, but that doesn't make them a master at it. In fact, most people who do that learn everything they need to know about their job in their first year and then repeat that same year of experience over and over again.

The best of the best keep learning, growing, and trying to improve. They have to do that because no matter who you are or what you do, if you're at the top, there's someone else who wants your spot.

In my lifetime, I've read thousands of books, and over the last fifteen years, I've written hundreds of columns and cranked out more than fifteen thousand blog posts, all of which have been publicly evaluated by commenters on social media and by the sheer number of people who were willing to read the post or ignore it. That's what it took for me to get good enough at writing to do it for a living.

What are you willing to put that kind of workload into to become successful at? That's the mentality you need to embrace if you want to become great at anything.

The great boxer Muhammad Ali once said, "The fight is won or lost far away from witnesses—behind the lines, in the gym, and out there on the road, long before I dance under those lights." It's not about shortcuts, lucky breaks, or secret tricks; it's about finding something you're willing to put that kind of effort into for month after month, year after year, until you master it.

72. First impressions are much more important than most people realize.

It's fine to say "Don't judge a book by its cover," but people are shallow and do it all day long.

The broker's office probably isn't hiring the guy with a neck tattoo, even if he's highly qualified. You might be the greatest guy in the world, but if you show up for your first date unshaven, wearing a T-shirt with a hole in it, it's probably going to be your last date. If you walk up behind someone at an ATM wearing a bandana and pants hanging down to your butt, it doesn't matter if you just finished singing in the church choir, the person is going to think you may rob him at any second.

It may be unfair that people form a lasting impression of you based on what they pick up within sixty seconds of meeting you, but they do.

The world's full of people who think you stink if you have bad breath that day. If you seem really quiet right off the bat, they'll assume you're shy. Talk too much? They'll believe you never shut up.

People also pay attention to grooming. Women tend to get this, but guys will walk around with a unibrow, hair sticking out of their nose, and fingernails bitten down to the nub and don't understand why the ladies are telling their friends to save them if you come over to talk.

Of course, I don't want to give the ladies too much credit. I know women who are gorgeous, except for the fact that they have greasy hair they don't bother to properly clean or style. I also used to have an adorable female friend who didn't understand why guys weren't interested. After she asked, I had to tell her it was because she dressed like a boy with loose-fitting clothing. If you want guys to look at you, then dress like you want guys to look at you. If you have curves, show them off. If you have weak spots, hide them. Don't wear a sleeveless dress if you have flabby arms. Clothes may not "make the man," but they make a big difference for both men and women.

There are whole books out there on body language, and they're worth reading because people will make judgments about you based on whether you hold your head high or low (high is better), how much space you take up (a lot shows confidence), and whether your posture is open (open shows you're more comfortable and confident) or closed. Most of the time, people don't even know they're doing it. Like animals, we've learned to read the signals and react to them.

When you're meeting someone for the first time, always try to put your best foot forward. Have a firm handshake. Leave your favorite dirty joke about the priest, the rabbi, and the Irishman who walk into a bar for another time. Get the details right because if you leave an impression, you need it to be a good one. That's how you get the job, the second date, or the invitation to the party. If you blow that opportunity to make a good first impression, you may never recover from it.

73. Make your habits, and your habits will make you.

Your life is a collection of habits. Are you fat or thin? Well, that depends on what you habitually eat. Are you educated or ignorant? That depends on whether you habitually study and grow. Can you cook? It depends on whether you've habitually made the effort to learn.

Have you saved money? Do you have good teeth? Are you flexible? Have you built up muscles at the gym? Can you run three miles? Do you have money saved? On and on it goes. It all depends on what your habits happen to be.

Show me someone who is outstanding at anything and I will show you someone who habitually works on it and tries to improve. That goes for the worst people at anything as well. How do people cross ethical lines into addiction, evil, tragedy, and disaster? One baby step at a time until they fall off the cliff.

Want to get fat? When you get stressed, habitually eat to release the tension. Want to end up in jail? Habitually break the law. Want to die of lung cancer at sixty-five? Habitually smoke. Want to crash your car, ruin your relationships, and die with liver failure at sixty? Habitually drink every day.

So what are your habits? What do you do every day just like you brush your teeth?

We've already talked about how compound interest can improve your life financially, but habitual effort in any area compounds the same way.

It's that twenty-fourth date, that thirty-second day in a row of not missing any exercise, that fifty-third time you go through a sparring session. One day, you're with a man who has feelings for you, and the next, he's in love and bound to you. One day you're exercising again even though you don't feel like it, and the next it's a habit. One day you're still just getting better at boxing, and the next, your footwork and combinations have finally clicked.

Then from there, as Charles Duhigg explains, other things start to happen.

"Take, for instance, studies from the past decade examining the impacts of exercise on daily routines. When people start habitually exercising, even as infrequently as once a week, they start changing other, unrelated patterns in their lives, often unknowingly. Typically, people who exercise start eating better and become more productive at work. They smoke less and show more patience with colleagues and family. They use their credit cards less frequently and say they feel less stressed. It's not completely clear why. But for many people, exercise is a keystone habit that triggers widespread change. 'Exercise spills over,' said James Prochaska, a University of Rhode Island researcher. 'There's something about it that makes other good habits easier.'"

As your habits change, you'll find your self-image starts to change along with it. So consciously make your habits, then let your habits make you.

74. Know when to hire outside help.

When you're dirt poor, you end up doing everything from working on your car to making household repairs to plumbing work yourself. Unfortunately, unless you are mechanically inclined, trying to MacGyver your way through every situation often doesn't work very well. Still, when you're poor, you don't feel like you have much of a choice.

As you get a little more money in your pocket, you realize that you can potentially hire people to do things you don't like to do. Not a fan of raking the yard, cleaning the house, or doing the cooking? Well, if you have money, honey, someone else has the time to get those chores done around your house. So, should you do it? There are three questions you need to answer first.

A. Are you even capable of doing it right? If you don't know how to do electrical work, pump out a septic tank, or paint, you probably don't want to try to learn it on the fly. Hire someone.

B. How much do you hate doing it? Believe it or not, I enjoy mowing the yard, so I do it myself. But raking the leaves? Cutting down trees? Doing a spring cleaning? I don't like doing those things at all, so I like to hire people to do those for me.

C. Is it worth your time? If you make $40 an hour, it's smarter to pay someone $20 an hour to spend all day working in your yard than it is for you to take a day off work and do it yourself.

You should also consider the fact that there are services online that let you hire people from all over the world to do virtual tasks. I used to take four to five hours of my time transcribing my interviews until I realized I could hire someone who can type 100 words a minute to do it for me for a reasonable price.

Additionally, I have a team of people in India who do all sorts of boring grunt work for my website that I don't want to do. They have a great work ethic, they follow directions, they work cheap, and they save me an enormous amount of time.

You can even hire virtual secretaries online. Do you need someone to do research for you? To manage your email? What if you don't need someone forty hours a week? Well, you can hire a virtual secretary online who can handle all of those things.

Getting back to the real world, you need to know when to hire a professional service and when to go cheap. Mowing the yard? Find some kid who'll do it for cheap. Cleaning your house? The professional maid services are expensive. Ask around and find some older woman who needs to make a few extra bucks every so often and hire her to clean. When you're talking about handymen, it's often difficult to find professional people. If you can find someone competent who shows up every time and doesn't charge a ridiculous amount, hang on to them. With mechanics, if you have serious work to do, then ask around at work or with your friends. Someone will be able to tell you about a shop that does quality work and won't rip you off. Failing that, take your vehicle to multiple places and get estimates. I once did that, and the first shop told me they needed to replace part of my engine for $300. I tried another place and they fixed the problem with a $6 hose. That's one heck of a savings just for being willing to check out a second place.

Save time and sometimes even money by learning when to hire people who can make life easier for you.

75. Learn to love problems.

If success were easy, everybody would do it. Because it's not, you have the opportunity to distinguish yourself by solving problems. The more problems you solve, the more success you'll have in life.

Then, once you're successful, you won't have any more problems, right? Wrong. But if you're lucky, you'll have a better class of problems.

What's a good problem? Having so many places that want to pay you money to write that you can't do them all. Dating four women and trying to settle on which one you like best. Having to hire an accountant and being stunned at how much you have to pay in taxes now that the money is rolling in.

Do you know how you end up with problems like that? You get there by solving lesser problems. In fact, you can tell the quality of a man's life by the quality of the problems that he has. Typically, high achievers have gotten so adept at problem solving that they can handle issues in short order that would turn the average person into a stressed-out, barely functional wreck.

On the other hand, some people spend *decades* stuck on the same problems. They fantasize about what it would be like if they had no problems. They wait for other people to fix their problems. They distract themselves any way they can to forget that they have a problem, but most of the time, their life doesn't start to improve until they start working to solve the problems they have so they can move on to new ones. Wouldn't you think it would work that way? After all, if you're an alcoholic, so poor you don't know where your next meal is coming from, or flunking out of school, it's hard to find better problems to solve because your current problem tends to be all-consuming.

The good news is that, as the great Albert Einstein said, "We cannot solve our problems with the same thinking we used when we created them." Put another way, you have to grow as a person to solve your problems. This is why you hear so many old people say, "I have no regrets." How can that be? Didn't they screw up? Sure. Didn't they have tough times? Absolutely they did. But to solve those problems, they had to become better and stronger. So as hard as it may seem sometimes, be appreciative of those challenges in your life because they are what will carve you into who you're supposed to become.

76. Almost everything is going to be harder than you think.

To be a human being, you have to be at least a little optimistic. After all, we're fragile creatures with an enormous number of easily damaged parts, yet we still drive, fly in airplanes, pet strange dogs on the head, and regularly socialize with other humans who are perfectly capable of killing us. Consider the fact that people do all sorts of activities that require them to wear helmets in order to lessen the chances that their head will be cracked open if they have an accident. Yet they do them anyway. That's optimism!

Unfortunately, this optimism regularly leads us to underestimate the difficulty and amount of time it will take to do just about everything.

How much time and effort will it take to get that promotion, get your new business off the ground, convince your future wife that she should marry you, get an A in that math class, or lose twenty-five pounds?

Probably considerably more than you're expecting.

When I started my website back in 2001, I was hoping it would take off within a year or two. Instead, it took four years for me to eke out enough revenue to make a living. Although I kept working hard and improving the website, nine years later, the page had only doubled in size. Two years after that, which was thirteen years after I started, traffic on an average day was twenty-five times higher than my previous totals with spikes as high as fifty times what I had done in an average day before.

That is life in a nutshell. You work, you work, you work, you can't believe you're working so hard, you work, you work, you work, you can't believe this is taking so long, you work, you work, and you work, and then you win.

It applies to everything from assembling a desk you bought at the furniture store to saving enough money to go on vacation to convincing your four-year-old son that there really aren't monsters in the closet that are going to eat him after you leave the room.

This is important, because one day when you're wondering if you're the only one going through hell who doesn't know anything else to do but to keep on going, it'll be good for you to know that you're not alone.

77. Losers make excuses for why they failed. Winners find ways to get the job done.

If you ever run your own business, let me promise that you will end up doing a lot of crap you don't want to do. When there's nobody else to fill in for someone who doesn't show up, you have to figure out a way to make it work. When there's an unpleasant situation nobody else can handle, you have to deal with it. When nobody knows what to do, you're the one who has to figure it out.

That makes a certain kind of sense to most people, but they forget that the same principle applies in their own lives. You're going to get kicked out if you don't have the money to pay the rent? Then you better borrow the money, take it out of savings, or convince the landlord to give you a little longer. Your marriage is falling apart and you want to stay together? You better be willing to talk it out, put in extra effort, go to therapy, or whatever else it takes to make it work. You're flunking out of college? Then get a tutor, go to a study group, or ask for extra credit.

Human beings have this tendency to assume that just because we don't know all the struggles and hard work that went into getting someone to the top, that there weren't any. We think someone who's smart, good looking, or athletically gifted had everything handed to him, but that's rarely true. In fact, when people do have those kinds of strokes of luck, they usually find that success slips through their fingers because they haven't done the preparation necessary for success. If you want to see a great example of that, according to a 2015 study by the Camelot Group, 44 percent of large lottery winners eventually go broke. How can that possibly be? It's because they have no idea what goes into creating or maintaining wealth, so when their pockets are finally filled with cash, they continue doing the same things that were keeping them from ever getting wealthy, except on a grander scale. They buy the mansion, collect cars, run up massive month-to-month expenses, and spend money like they can't ever run out . . . until they do.

What you have to accept is that whether you succeed or fail is all on your shoulders. Proudly accept that responsibility and do what it takes to get the job done. That's what winners do.

Sure, it's fun to fantasize about getting all the glory, acclaim, and power of winning without having to do all the hard work, but as college coach Fielding Yost once said, "The will to win is worthless if you do not have the will to prepare."

As someone who's actually sparred, I can tell you "heart" doesn't mean anything when you're getting punched in the face every few seconds because you're gassed while you can't land a shot because your opponent has done a lot more cardio than you. Unless you get lucky in that situation, you and your giant heart are going to get knocked on your behind.

You want to get an A in a college course? Attend all the lectures. Do your homework. Join a study group. Start reviewing the material a week early instead of the night before the test.

Do you have to give a speech? If you want it to be good, you better set aside some time to write it and practice it.

Do you want to impress your boss with a report that you're hoping will lead to a promotion? Well, that promotion probably depends as much on how much time you put into it as it does on how good the information turns out to be.

Losers forego all of this and embrace the magical words of failure, "It's not fair!" They complain that someone else has it easier. They make a half-hearted effort, give up, and then say, "I tried." They'll work until it gets hard, confusing, or uncomfortable, and then they throw up their hands. They wait for someone else—their wife, their pastor, the government—anybody to come in and fix problems they should be handling themselves.

There's an easy, easy way to know if you're a winner or a loser. Think about the parts of your life you're unhappy with and ask yourself who's responsible for your problems. Winners end up pointing the finger at themselves, and then they do something about it. Losers point the finger elsewhere. It's their kids, their husband, their boss, their mom, bad luck, rich people, liberals, society—that's all crap.

"No, John, you don't understand, you see . . ."

Just stop because I do understand. You may have had a bad break. Other people may have done awful things to you. You might have horrible luck. It's still your responsibility to fix it. If that's too hard to deal with, then winning is too hard to deal with because that's the attitude winners take.

Understand that I am not telling you this to hurt your feelings or be mean to you. I am telling you this because I want you to have a good life. The easiest thing in the world is to shift the blame to someone else, and the hardest is to take personal responsibility for your own failings. You know, the ones you're ashamed of, the ones that make you feel bad, the ones that make you hurt? However, the unfortunate truth is doing that is a prerequisite for success. Change your attitude; stop passing the buck and you'll start passing other people up!

Chapter 10

BE RESPONSIBLE

78. Nobody owes you a living.

Your life is your responsibility and not just because it's the right thing to do, but because the hard truth is that no one other than you and *maybe* your family cares.

The average person cares more about what they will be having for lunch today than how your college loans will be paid for, the terrible medical diagnosis you just got, or how your girlfriend dumped you for the drummer in an AC/DC cover band.

That's because people are too busy taking care of themselves and their families to worry about your problems. Sure, they may feel a burst of genuine pity for you after they hear your tale of woe, but then they'll be right back on their cell phones trying to get to the next level on the game they're playing five minutes after you walk away.

Oh, but what about the government? Do you really want its help? Do you want to feel all those eyes burning into your back when you whip out those food stamps? Do you want to live in crummy government housing? Do you want to jump through whatever hoops some dead-eyed bureaucrat comes up with so you can get just enough help to stay poor and miserable? Is that the sort of person you admire? Is that the one you grew up wanting to be? You should want more out of life than what the government is willing to give to you in return for your pride.

Speaking as someone who's gone a week on potatoes and dollar burritos, who once slept in an elevator overnight rather than take charity, and who seriously considered living in his own car for a couple of months at one point to save money, I can tell you that taking responsibility for your life is worth it. Not only does it give you some great stories, it teaches you that you can make it when times get tough. Perhaps more importantly, it keeps you ferociously motivated to make sure that you don't stay behind the eight ball. When you know it's up to you to solve your own problems, you learn to do what it takes to get the job done.

Be that person, the one who takes care of himself and doesn't expect anyone else to step in and save his bacon when he makes a mistake or times get tough. You'll never regret it

79. If you can't support yourself, you shouldn't have a child or get married.

Money isn't everything, but you do not want to get married or have a kid when you're so poor you're walking around the Dollar Store wishing you had the money to buy something.

Sure, you can be a great parent or have a great marriage when you're dirt poor—and many, many people do.

Unfortunately, financial pressure can also destroy a marriage because it turns every trip to the grocery store or night out into a point of conflict.

Who wants to come home to "Seriously, did you buy a steak? We can't afford that" or "I know you really want to go out, but we don't have the money. You should have thought of that before you gave your mother a $50 birthday gift!"

I had a friend of mine who explicitly told me that he divorced his wife because money was tight and she kept blowing all the cash he was trying to save up. Would they have still been together if they were making another $20,000 a year? Maybe, maybe not, but it's entirely possible that if you took those financial pressures off the relationship, they might have been fine.

This is something to think about if you're thinking of having a kid or getting married young before you start making any real money. Sure, the idea of "getting married and saving money by sharing expenses" may sound appealing, but you're also sharing debts, bills, and bad financial decisions.

And kids? They're *ridiculously* expensive. You have to pay for their food, their toys, their bed, their clothing, school expenses, day care, babysitters—it goes on and on.

What you really don't want to do is to get so far in the hole that you end up on government assistance. Then both of you feel bad about it; you worry about the lessons you're teaching your kids when they get hand outs, and you're still miserable because it's not like the government is giving you a mansion with a Rolls Royce to ferry you around.

At the end of the day, it's a lot easier to say that "Money doesn't matter because all you need is love" than it is to live by that philosophy.

80. Don't risk killing yourself by driving when you're so tired you can barely hold your eyes open; take a cat nap.

Once, I was already sleep deprived and had to drive from Raleigh to Charlotte, North Carolina, after midnight. It was a three-hour drive and I was so tired I barely knew where I was. I tried cranking up the music, driving with the window down, and stopping to get a sugary beverage, but nothing worked. I was getting so sleepy that the waking and dreaming world were starting to merge a bit. At one point, for a couple of seconds, I thought there was a dinosaur in the road until I snapped out of it. Eventually, I did make it home, and then I was horrified when I realized that I literally didn't remember the last hour and a half of the drive. I don't even know how that's possible. Was I doing the equivalent of sleep walking at the wheel? Either way, I made it home alive. Not everyone does. A nephew of mine fell asleep at the wheel, ran off the road, and crashed. His vehicle caught fire and he later died of his injuries. Either of the two of us could have just as easily crossed the median, hit someone head-on, and killed both them and us.

These days, when I get in that position, I have some different options. I react well to 5-hour Energy, and oftentimes, taking a shot of that gets the job done. If I'm *really* tired, I get a hotel room for the night. However, if I don't want to spend all night at some hotel in the middle of nowhere and I don't have a ridiculous drive left, I will pull my car over, crawl into the backseat, and go to sleep.

I've done that on the side of the road before, but I'm not a huge fan of sleeping a few feet from where thousands of other cars that may be driven by other sleepy people or drunks will be passing.

So instead, I like to look for big parking lots, shopping centers, Walmarts, or even hotels. Is that safe? Maybe not as safe as your own bed, but given that it's a public area, you're probably not in danger unless you're pulling over in a crummy part of town. (Hint: If you have to ask the gangbangers on the corner where the best place to pull over and go to sleep would be, you should keep on moving.) After I find one of those parking lots, I find a spot that is as dark and out of the way as possible, lock the car, and sleep. I've found that even thirty to sixty minutes of sleep is usually enough to wake me up again for a few hours.

If that gets you to your destination an hour later than planned, that's not ideal, but it sure beats dying on the way home.

81. If you buy a gun, learn to use it.

As the old saying goes, "When seconds count, the police are only minutes away." In a situation like that, where your life or the life of your family is in danger and a weapon may be the difference between life and death, it can be useful to have a gun. However, if you haven't been trained to use a gun, it can be worse than useless.

You might not even know how to release the safety. Even if you do, the gun might jam, you might not know how to clear it, and then you're standing there helpless in front of an angry robber who knows you tried to kill him. Alternately, if you don't know what you're doing, you might miss. Missing with a gun can be dangerous because that bullet can go right through the wall and into your kid or right out the window, into your neighbor Jim's head. If you haven't been trained with a weapon, you may have never even realized how much it mattered what's *behind* the person you're shooting at, but it can be a life-changing mistake.

If you and your family are safely locked in your bedroom and someone is ransacking your living room, should you confront him or stay in your bedroom? (Stay put.) Did you know that? Do you know when you need to inform an officer that you have a gun in your car and when you don't? (It depends on the state.)

I'm not telling you this to convince you not to get a gun. To the contrary, I believe guns are like life insurance. You hope you never need it, but if you need one and don't have it, you're screwed.

Personally, I do have a gun and I spent a week getting trained on how to use it at one of the best firearm training institutes in the world. I'm not a gun nut like some of my friends, and I can't tell you the ins and outs of every firearm out there. However, I definitely know my way around a Glock 19, which is what I have. I know how to shoot accurately with it; I know how to clear it when it has been jammed, and I know when I should and shouldn't use it. I genuinely hope I never have to kill anyone with it, but I have spent enough time training with it to be comfortable saying that if it's you or me, it will probably be you. If you have a gun, you should feel the same way.

In westerns, spy thrillers, and policy buddy dramas, people are shot all the time with few consequences. In the real world, every time you pull the trigger, it has the potential to change your life and the life of whomever may end up on the business end of the bullet you fire. Take that seriously and train yourself so you don't end up being one of those cautionary tales people tell about knuckleheads who are irresponsible with their gun.

82. Prepare a will, a medical directive, and a listing of what sort of arrangements you want made if you die.

It's hard to believe when you're young but yes, you too are going to die one day. Happily, it probably won't be soon.

Probably.

If it is soon, it's going to be a shockwave in the life of everyone who knows you. I hate to say this, but when someone who's old dies, especially if she's lived a good life, it's hard to feel too bad for her unless you're closely related. When some eighty-year-old who had a beautiful marriage, five kids, and twelve grandkids passes on, people tend to think, "That was a life well lived. I hope I do that well." When a twenty-five-year-old dies, it's "How tragic that his life was cut short before he ever reached his potential!"

In any case, if you pass away, it's worth remembering that funerals are ridiculously expensive. If whomever would be handling it doesn't have deep pockets, you better have life insurance or you could put that person in a tough financial position. On the upside, when you're young, life insurance is cheap.

You also need to have a will. You have a shotgun and $5,000 in a savings account? Well, who gets that? If you have a dog, who do you want to take care of him after you're gone? If you have any real assets, it's essential that you do this because I've seen this issue turn whole families against each other. Somebody dies, and a year later, they're at everyone's throat over who got a piece of furniture or a house. If they're going to get mad at anyone, let them get mad at you. You'll be dead. It won't matter.

Additionally, what if you don't die but are incapacitated? Do you want to live on in a vegetative state, or do you want someone to pull the plug? Again, this issue can tear families apart. You don't want your sister and your brother fighting likes cats and dogs because one of them wants to "put you out of your misery" and the other one feels like that's murder. It's your life. You make the decision.

Last but not least, what kind of arrangements do you want, if any? Do you know that neither my parents nor I want a funeral service after we die—and no, we're not part of some weird religious cult. The idea of a bunch of people showing up somewhere to be sad because we're gone doesn't appeal to us. If you feel that way, then you better make it clear or you'll be having a service after you're gone. If you do want a service, do you have any special requests? My brother had Lynyrd Skynyrd's "Freebird" played at his funeral. Is there a song you want played? After you die, do you want to be buried or cremated? If you're getting buried, where do you want to be buried? If you're cremated, what do you want done with the ashes?

Thinking about what happens after you die can be unpleasant and even a little frightening, but a couple of hours' work on your part now may make life a lot easier on your family after you die. Losing you will be enough stress on them as it is; don't add to it by refusing to do your due diligence in handling your own demise. You may not have come into this world on your own terms, but if you plan well enough, you can leave on your own terms.

83. At a minimum, keep a basic to-do list.

When you're in high school, typically you have whoever's taking care of you giving you reminders twenty-three times a day. Then you go to school where you have assigned classes and duties, and if you miss them, someone will ask about it.

As I found out when I became an adult, life didn't quite work that way. More than once, I realized I hadn't paid my utility bill by having my power cut off. Ideally, you should set your bills up to be paid automatically, but if you can't afford it, at least have someplace you put all your bills as they come in.

As to budgeting, after kiting a couple of checks for pizza, my local pizza place would no longer deliver to my house. It wasn't intentional. I just didn't have a handle on how much money I had in my bank account. You don't want to realize that you have no money left for food for the next two weeks because you spent it all getting your car detailed.

Incidentally, as I got older, I started paying more attention to that kind of thing and it turned out to be valuable because I did have someone run up charges on my debit card. They were five states away from me buying stuff at a grocery store. Had my bank's loss control department not recognized the suspicious purchases, I still would have caught it later that night when I checked, before they started buying TVs and computers with *my money*. If you are not looking at your bank account every day, you are vulnerable.

You also need a place to write down everything in your schedule. Got a doctor's appointment? Write it down. Are you taking your sister out to lunch next week? Write it down. Have you planned a once-in-a-lifetime party in three weeks when your parents are out of town? Write it down, or don't be surprised if dozens of drunken partygoers turn up at your house while you're getting sloshed across town with your weird friend Ed, whom you only went out with because you had nothing better to do.

You also need a to-do list. It doesn't have to be fancy. If you want to make it fancy, put the most important things at the top and the least important things at the bottom. You can also add in dates to make yourself feel ashamed that you've been planning to clean out the garage for four months now and are still too lazy to get around to doing it.

Children get told what to do by their parents. Adults have to do some planning to make sure their life goes smoothly.

84. There is safety in numbers.

As a chivalrous southern gentleman, I think rapists deserve the death penalty, and if we didn't have a clause in the Constitution forbidding cruel and unusual punishment, I'd like it to be as slow and painful as possible. I also think it's absolutely wrong to blame women who've been raped. It doesn't matter what you're wearing or if you changed your mind at the last minute; the fault lies with the rapist.

All that being said, the best piece of advice young women are *ever* going to get about avoiding rape is not to end up alone somewhere with a guy or around a bunch of guys, drunk. When you get in that position, especially if you're sloppy drunk, you are in danger.

Once when I was a freshman in college, I walked into my dorm room at two a.m., and on *my bed* was a busty, attractive woman I barely knew. She was wasted, and the first words out of her mouth were "Please f*** me. Please, please f*** me." I could have locked the door, had my way with her, and what would I have probably been telling myself in the morning? "She was in my bed. She *asked* me to do it." Fortunately for her, I recognized that she was nearly blackout drunk, and I'm not that kind of guy. You don't ever want to be in a position where you have to rely on the decency of strangers to keep something terrible from happening to you.

Incidentally, if I wanted to go into detail about women I personally know who have been raped, I could add a half-dozen other stories, almost all of them involving copious amounts of alcohol. That certainly doesn't excuse what the rapists did, but there is a lesson there if you want to avoid being raped.

I'm not telling you to avoid alcohol or sex, but I am telling you that if you're a woman and you're going to get hammered, you *better* have someone you trust looking out for you or you may live to regret it.

Chapter 11

SELF-AWARENESS

85. You are not a victim.

Oh no, someone called you a name! You think you're disadvantaged because of an "ism." It's not fair that you got into a nasty conflict with someone else and came out on the short end of the stick. You're a victim! You need someone to pity you so people will show up and fix your problems!

This is going to be hard for some of you to hear, but that's loser talk.

If you live in America at the time this book is written, not only are you better off than the vast majority of people living today, you're doing better than 99.9 percent of the human beings who ever lived. Throughout most of human history, the wretched masses barely made enough to live, had little freedom, and found life to be, in the immortal words of Thomas Hobbes, "Nasty, brutish and short." Right now, half the people reading this book learned about it on the Internet, then had it shipped to their house where they sit on a plush bed in an air-conditioned room, snacking on the cheap, delicious snacks they received from a nearby supermarket while they drink a cool, refreshing beverage they grabbed out of their refrigerator while they enjoy the book. Many of the advances that have revolutionized human existence only became widely available in the last hundred years, and *you* have access to them while the richest, most privileged people on earth a hundred years ago had nothing that could compare.

You think you have it hard? Compared to whom? Some poor schmo in a totalitarian country who barely has enough to eat and can be imprisoned or shot if he offends the wrong government official or can't manage to save up enough for a bribe on the dollar per day that he makes?

Don't ever feel sorry for yourself. Don't ever seek pity from other people. Don't ever play the victim, even if you are one.

Why? It's a mentality. If you wait for someone else to solve your problems, you're usually in for a long wait. Even if you do get help, you probably won't like the help you get.

That's why you're almost always better off asking yourself what you can learn from every situation and then pulling yourself up by your own bootstraps.

You don't think you make enough in your job? Add some new skills and ask for a raise. Your boss won't give it to you even though you deserve it? Get another job. Someone calls you a name? Ignore him because if you don't respect him, what difference does it make? If that doesn't work, learn to fight back. You think someone isn't treating you with respect? Demand it.

It's not always fun to take total responsibility for your own life, and there are times when it seems easier to do anything else—but if you want to live up to your full potential and have the kind of life you dream of, that's what you need to do.

86. Ask yourself if it's the right thing to do.

My own dear mother told me the best piece of life advice she ever received was from a policeman named Bill Shockley. Someone was asking him what he thought he should do in a particular situation, and Bill's response was, "Is it the right thing to do?"

Obviously, in his line of work, there are a lot of people who could have used that advice before they kicked an old lady down the stairs so they could steal her welfare check or got so drunk that they didn't realize they were trying to mug someone in front of the police station.

However, this is a piece of advice that you will often find to be applicable in your own life even though you aren't a criminal (hopefully).

Do you go to the funeral even though you don't feel like it? When you need money and you pick up a twenty off the ground that someone didn't realize they'd dropped, do you give them the money back? When you promise your kid that you're going to go to his baseball game but you're having a great time talking to your friends, do you break away and go? When you give your word, do you honor it even though it's inconvenient and the person you gave it to isn't in a position to force you to do it? When nothing would be easier than to go along with everyone else who's doing the wrong thing, do you want to be the one person who speaks out and says, "We can't do this?"

Over time, these little decisions shape and mold your character. Whether you're able to believe that you're a good person or not will probably be based on how you perform in these situations. As the great John Wooden said, "The true test of a man's character is what he does when no one is watching." Even evil people hear that little voice of their conscience; they've just gotten good at ignoring it. Will you ignore it or will you listen to it? Will you do the right thing only when it's easy, or will you stick with it when it gets hard? Over time, whether you "do the right thing" in these little moments of decision will define you as a person. Make sure you can be proud of how you're defined.

87. Here's how to make a decision.

A lot of people struggle with making decisions. They delay and delay and delay and delay and delay (you get the idea) and then finally, they sort of choose, then go back the other way, and a month later, they still don't know what they're going to do.

Do you want to know the *right way* to make fast, effective decisions that you don't have to revisit?

Well, first off, you need to understand yourself. You need to know what you want out of life, what your goals and your dreams are. I know, I know, most of you are reading that and going, "Oh, I need to map out my entire life. Well, let me jump right on that after lunch!"

Actually, you should jump right on that after lunch because most people have trouble making decisions because they don't know what they want in the first place. The better you know yourself, the easier it becomes to make even huge, life-changing decisions. On the other hand, to paraphrase Lewis Carroll, "If you don't care where you're going, then it doesn't matter which way you go."

Once you know what you want to do in the first place, you begin the normal decision-making process most people engage in. You come up with pluses and minuses, consult your head and your heart, and make your call. The reason this process often doesn't produce good results is that most people don't know what they want in the first place, but they also don't know what to do after they've made a decision.

Once you make your decision, you don't revisit it unless new information comes in. If you dumped your girlfriend because she's mentally unstable, don't change your mind and take her back two weeks later if nothing has changed. On the other hand, if she tells you she's finally decided to go to therapy, then you can at least think things through again. If you decided not to buy a car because it's too pricey, don't reconsider your decision three weeks later unless you notice the car is deeply discounted or you get some huge unexpected bonus at work. If you commit to spending two hours of quality time per night playing with your son, don't give it up because there's something on TV that you want to see. On the other hand, if after a month, you decide your decision is stretching you too far and something has to give, then consider cutting back to an hour.

This is an important concept because without doing this, you never make final decisions. Today you feel one way, but tomorrow you may feel another and change your mind. If you never firmly decide, can you even be said to have made a decision in the first place?

88. Trust your instincts.

How does a wolf pack coordinate well enough to bring down a deer without talking? How do the swallows know to go back to Capistrano? How do salmon know to go upstream to spawn? Why does your dog sniff another dog's butt like it's soaked in his favorite fragrance?

Instinct.

We human beings are not as in tune with our instincts as animals because those impulses are socialized out of us so we can be part of a civilization.

The problem with that is that you have access to more information than your conscious mind can process. Subconsciously, you're watching body language and microexpressions, catching minimal changes in tone, and simultaneously evaluating dozens of pieces of information you don't have time to think about.

Your instincts tap into all this information and make it available to you if you choose to use it.

Unfortunately, your instincts don't give you a lot of detail. You get a vague feeling about something, one that's easy to overlook if you aren't used to paying attention to your instincts.

Do you have a feeling deep down in your gut that—

- It's not safe to be alone with someone?
- Someone is lying to you?

- You shouldn't agree to a business deal?
- What you're about to do is a huge mistake?
- It's not safe to go somewhere?
- A person is someone who's going to be trouble down the line?
- You shouldn't get in a car?

If so, then pay attention to it.

You still have to do your homework. Study up. Be logical. Know the situation inside and out, but listen to what your intuition is telling you because it can see things you don't. At the very least, if your intuition is telling you to be careful, you should get your antenna up.

I don't know how many times I've heard people say something like "I knew something wasn't right" or "I got a bad feeling about it," right before they describe some horrible thing that happened to them that they could have prevented if they'd listened to their gut. Trust your instincts and don't let that happen to you.

89. You will likely find that your parents are right about a lot more than you think.

When you're young, your parents seem like superheroes because they can do all the things you can't do. They're not afraid of monsters under the bed, they can drive, and they know *everything*. You know they know *everything* because you ask! Why is the sky blue? What's an aardvark? Why is that man black? Is it because he's covered with chocolate? (Yes, I did once say this loudly in public when I was about four, albeit to my embarrassed grandfather, not my parents.)

Then you get into your late teens (practically an adult!) and your parents don't seem so smart anymore. Your dad has no idea who the coolest new bands are, your mother doubts that you'll be a famous guitarist (of course you will), and both of them always shoot down your great ideas like staying out as late as you want or skipping school whenever you have a test you didn't study for at all.

Suddenly, you start to think you've learned all you need to know from your parents.

Not so.

Your parents may be different from you. They may not have an IQ as high as yours. They may be deeply flawed individuals, but unless they molested you, they're psychopaths, or they're evil people, there's still a lot you can learn from them.

That's because if you're young, they have something you don't: experience.

They've worked a crummy job similar to the one you're thinking of taking. They know someone who had the same type of marriage problem you're going through, and they know what they did to solve it. They had a cousin who had a weird rash like you do and can tell you what she did to clear it up.

That doesn't mean your parents are always right, and God knows that talking to them about some of the issues you have in your life isn't always easy, but they can be invaluable sounding boards.

If I need investment advice? The first person I go to is my father. My mother knows everything there is to know about fixing up a house. If I have a question about whether I need an electrician, how to hang curtains, or what type of tile I need for my kitchen, she knows the answer or at least who to ask. Is my car doing something weird? My father can make an educated guess as to what's wrong with it. If I have an accounting question related to my business, my mother has it down cold.

Your parents may not know the same things as my parents, but they know a lot, and if you're their child, they're going to be willing to share what they know. Take advantage of it while you can because, as my mother says, "When someone dies, all the experience and skills he learned over the course of a lifetime dies with him."

90. Push yourself harder than anyone else does, but also forgive yourself.

You are probably going to have few people in your life who are going to care if you succeed or fail, and most of them aren't going to want to risk being too blunt.

If they think you dress like a hobo, need to stop drinking so much, or should stop watching cartoons all day and get a job, they may hem and haw, make subtle suggestions, and hint at what they really mean, but seldom will they be 100 percent truthful with you.

Because of this, if you're going to achieve your full potential, you have to be your own harshest critic. As Henry Ward Beecher said, "Hold yourself responsible for a higher standard than anybody else expects of you. Never excuse yourself. Never pity yourself. Be a hard master to yourself, and be lenient to everybody else." Show me anyone who's really good at anything and I'll show you someone who relentlessly works on improving.

Many people can't handle this because they don't understand how to critique themselves properly. They fail and, instead of examining their mistake and figuring out how to improve, they tell themselves that they're a loser who never does anything right. Some people spend a lifetime kicking themselves over one mistake they made.

If someone talked to a friend of yours like that, you'd punch them in the nose. Yet you'll talk to yourself like that and tell yourself that it's motivational. Back in the real world, when you do that, you become depressed and give up.

This is why you have to forgive yourself for your mistakes. Let your failures motivate you, teach you, and show you where you need to improve, but don't use them as an excuse to beat yourself up.

This is going to be hard for you to believe if you're not familiar with the concept, but you always do the best you can, given your knowledge level, your experience, and your training. Accept where you are, accept where you fall short, forgive yourself for your shortcomings, and push yourself to the limit. When you can strive to be your best without fear of a harsh judgment from yourself for falling short, you will be shocked at the progress you can make.

91. Few things in life have any intrinsic meaning.

There's a story that I have always loved that's supposedly all about luck, but it really describes a way of looking at life.

There was an old farmer who worked his crops for many years. One day his horse ran away. Upon hearing the news, his neighbors came to visit. "Such bad luck," they said sympathetically.

"Maybe," the farmer replied. The next morning the horse returned, bringing with it three other wild horses. "How wonderful," the neighbors exclaimed.

"Maybe," replied the old man. The following day, his son tried to ride one of the untamed horses, was thrown off, and broke his leg. The neighbors again came to offer their sympathy on his misfortune. "Maybe," answered the farmer.

The day after, military officials came to the village to draft young men into the army. Seeing that the son's leg was broken, they passed him by. The neighbors congratulated the farmer on how well things had turned out.

"Maybe," said the farmer.

Life is often like this. A humiliating defeat can inspire you to work so hard that you become better than ever. An incredible stroke of fortune can make you so complacent and arrogant that you fail. So how good or bad are most events in your life?

Couple that with the fact that few things in life have an intrinsic meaning. Take funerals, for example. Most of us mourn when someone dies. In other cultures, they celebrate. When you think of someone leaving all the troubles of this world behind and going to heaven, we could easily choose to be happy about that as well.

Imagine being in terrible pain. There's nothing good about that, right? Maybe. On the other hand, if you're in pain because you had an operation that will allow you to see for the first time or that ends a painful limp you've had all your life, it's easy to see how it could be a good thing that you're in pain.

When you have something happen to you, make the assumption that there is a benevolent force in the universe that wants you to be better, stronger, and happier. Look at whatever troubles you have in light of that and ask yourself if there's a better interpretation of what's happening to you.

Did your girlfriend dump you? Maybe that's freeing you up to find someone better. Did you wreck your car but walk away from it? Maybe you needed to go through that to learn to be more careful so you could avoid a worse accident later. Did you get a D in your freshman calculus class? Maybe that's a way to teach you that you need to buckle down and study harder next semester.

When you start reframing your problems in this way, you'll find you have a lot less to be unhappy about than you think.

Chapter 12

LIVE LIFE TO THE FULLEST

92. Get out there and live!

It may be hard to believe if you're young, but all those old people you see hobbling around? They were young once, like you. And like them, you too are going to get old, and yes, one day you are going to die.

Today, it may seem like you have all the time in the world, but one day the sand is going to start running down in your hourglass and the things that matter today aren't going to seem important.

What's going to matter are the people you connected with during your life: your friends, your family, and the people you love. You're going to look back at the dreams you had during your life and you're going to wonder how many of them you accomplished. You're going to think about the potential you had, the things you could have done with your life—and you're going to judge yourself on how many of them you accomplished.

Anaïs Nin once said, "People living deeply have no fear of death." Is that going to be you, or are you going to be terrified when your time comes because all your hopes, all your dreams, all the things you wanted to do and the people you wanted to love are still inside you, pining to come out?

Are you doing what you want to do in life, or are you stuck doing things you don't want to do and watching a few hours' worth of TV every night to kill the pain? Have you at least made an attempt to mend that broken relationship with someone you used to be tight with? Have you said "I love you" to someone who matters today? Don't go to the grave with the best part of your life still inside of you. Do something about it now, today, while you can. Be happy with what you earn and accomplish, but find someone you want to share it with.

A man with legendary accomplishments and infinite riches is still poor indeed if he has no one to share it with.

93. When in doubt, act!

When you look back at the great moments of your life, you're not going to think of that time you slept in, binge watched an old TV show, or blew off a party with your friends to play video games.

Take a moment and think about the best moments of your life. Didn't almost all of them happen when you were out doing something? Wasn't it when you made the move on a girl, were having a great time at a party, were cheered by a crowd, or were on vacation looking at a breathtakingly beautiful natural scene? I can't tell you what your greatest moments were, but I can tell you that they probably involved something that put you in motion. A person in motion tends to stay in motion while a person sitting on the couch tends to stay right there until the cushion matches the shape of his butt.

. . . Which brings us back to everyday life. You'll get those opportunities to go do something and you'll be torn. You *might* have a good time, but inertia keeps you rooted in place and you're tempted to stay in. Should you go out? Should you not? You're not sure. Everybody's been there, right?

Well, when you get to that place, *always, always, always* have a bias toward action because that's where the memories are made, where you get experience, and how you become an interesting person. You want to meet some new people? Do you want to do something intriguing instead of the same old, same old? Do you want women to look at you and think, "Wow, I want to be part of that guy's life because it seems exciting"?

Then day after day, time after time, you have to choose action over inertia. So, if you're on the bubble about whether you should do something or not, do it by default. Have that bias toward action because life is in the doing!

94. Keep balance in these six key areas of your life: health, career, romantic, social, money, and religion.

One of the most difficult things about being human is that there are so many different areas that you have to work on to be successful. Even if you excel beyond 99.9 percent of human beings in an area or two, you can still feel like an unhappy failure.

If you're a billionaire but no woman would ever talk to you if you weren't rich, how happy are you? If you have a half dozen close friends and everyone loves your company, but you're impotent and three hundred pounds overweight, is that how you want to live your life? If you look like a Greek god but nobody likes you because you smell bad and obsessively rant about cheese, do you feel good about where you're at in life?

The good news is we can be happy, even if we have areas in our life that are deficient, but the bad news is that our weak areas are weak for a reason, and they tend to have an outsized impact on our lives. If you're not pleased with the quality of your life, you are probably falling down in one of these six areas.

Health: Are you fat or thin? Out of shape or in shape? Are there things you want to do but can't because of your physical condition? Do you spend a significant amount of time feeling bad because of your health?

Career: Are you happy with what you do for a living? Does it challenge you? Are you advancing? Does it pay the bills?

Romantic: Are you dating, married, or single? Are you happy with whatever your status may be? Are you in love with someone who loves you? Are you able to attract the sort of partner you want?

Social: Do you have any good friends? Do you have people you can hang out with? Are there people you can spend time with in person as opposed to just talking to them online?

Money: Do you have enough money set aside to take care of a big surprise bill? How about enough to live for six months if you lost your job? Do you have the money you need to buy the things you want and do the things you want to do?

Religion: Do you believe in God? Do you talk to Him regularly? Do you feel like He has a role in your life? Do you believe He loves you and has a plan for you? Do you feel "right" with the Lord?

If you feel a sense of rumbling discontent in your life, ask yourself these questions to help pinpoint what's causing it. Happiness is relative, and even if you are mediocre in some of these areas, you can still enjoy life; however, those weak spots will keep you from being as happy as you can be. Unfortunately, if you put more effort into addressing the places you're lacking, you may start to slip in other areas. That's the great challenge we all face, and it's a big part of what makes life so complex. That's a good thing, though. If life weren't harsh and uncertain, it wouldn't be meaningful.

95. Don't major in minor things.

There are an infinite number of things you can do with your time. I once had a roommate who absolutely mastered a video game. There's nothing wrong with that per se, but in his case, the price of that mastery was spending several hours a night obsessively playing the game *for months*. I guess that might make sense if he was going to be playing the game professionally, but is that the best use of, let's say, 360 hours of your life?

Before you laugh at him, how often do you check your social media?

How many times per day do you check your email or cell phone? Every time you hear a beep? If you're spending hours per day checking your phone and social media (and many of you are), what do you get out of that exactly? If you did it three times a day, would you be better or worse off? If your friends didn't get an immediate response because you were shopping for groceries or chatting in person with a friend, would it hurt anything?

Are you doing the things that are important in life, or is this the sixth day in a row you've planned and failed to clean out your closet? Are you spending the majority of your time doing the things that are essential to you, or are you frittering away your time channel surfing? Are you spending your days making progress toward your goals or incessantly working on urgent but unimportant busy work? Look back at the past week and ask yourself: did I accomplish anything important?

There's an old Roman saying that you should never forget: *Every hour wounds and the last one kills.*

The most valuable thing you personally own isn't your car, your house, or your TV; it's your time. What you do with it day to day will determine the quality of your life and what you accomplish before you die. Use it poorly, and one day, when you're lying on your deathbed, you'll think back to the years you spent majoring in minor things and you will deeply regret it.

96. The quality of your life can be greatly increased by cutting things away from it.

The first impulse most people have when they want to improve their lives is to add things to it—more exercise, more friends, more activities, more projects. Too much is never enough!

The problem with this is that there is only one of you and there are only so many hours in a day. If you keep adding in new activities, at some point you're going to get overloaded. At that point, "too much is never enough" can turn into "too much of a good thing."

Now you would think that it would be easy to cut unproductive activities out of your schedule, but that's not always so. Sometimes we're reluctant to admit that we've sunk time, money, or effort into an activity that wasn't worth doing. Other times, we hate to tell someone "no" or worry that we'll disappoint a friend. We can just continue to do unproductive things out of a sense of habit.

This is a mistake. Not only do you need to safeguard your time, you also have to consider the opportunity cost. Any time and money you waste on an unproductive activity is time and money that could have been better spent.

Now, even though it may not be easy, what I've just told you probably makes a certain kind of sense. However, the next step is one that few people typically consider unless someone points it out to them.

Oftentimes, especially if you are a busy, highly productive person, you can benefit from cutting *useful* activities out of your schedule to make time for even more important activities.

To give you a personal example, my website Rightwingnews.com has been my bread and butter over the years. However, I've created a number of other websites as well. I had a website dedicated to videos, to pictures, and to quotes. All of them took time and money to produce, and I liked how all of the websites turned out. Unfortunately, those websites weren't catching on and I had a decision to make. Did I keep pouring time, money, and effort into websites that weren't having much success or stay focused on the website I had that was taking off? I chose to do the latter, and eventually *Right Wing News* pulled in more than fifteen million readers a month.

Don't be afraid of change, afraid to say "no," or afraid to slice activities away from your schedule until you're maximizing the value of your time by spending most of it doing important things. Your time is precious. Treat it that way.

97. If you're not going to remember it in five years, it doesn't matter.

Life is full of minor annoyances. Your boss says something that makes you worry you'll get fired, you have a fight with a friend, your kid gets mad at you, your favorite team loses the Super Bowl, you're late to work—it goes on and on. The most common one these days is "Someone I don't know said something mean to me on the Internet!" These little annoyances spoil your day, and for many people, they can spoil their whole week.

When you become emotionally affected by these problems, ask yourself if you're going to remember them in five years. Maybe the answer will be yes. Going to your grandpa's funeral, putting your dog down, or breaking both your legs in a car wreck tends to stick with you for a while.

However, most of the other things that you obsess over and worry about won't even be significant next week, much less in five years.

That big fight with your girlfriend will likely blow over, your cat's injured leg will probably get better, and chances are you won't lose your job—but even if you do, you'll still be fine. That might sound a little Pollyanna-ish, but isn't that the way it works in the real world? Ninety-five percent of the things you worry about either don't happen or aren't as bad as you thought they'd be.

That's going to be true throughout your whole life. You're going to fret, you're going to get upset, you're going to worry yourself sick—and a week later you'll barely even remember why. If you're going to do that, at least save it for something that matters.

98. Continue learning.

As the great Ray Kroc once said, "When you're green, you're growing. When you're ripe, you rot." If that's not quite getting the idea across, recognize that there's also a lot of truth to that old saying, *Happiness is growth*.

You *need* to grow as a human being to be happy and successful. If you're young, growth has happened in your life almost by default. You learn; you go to high school; you meet new friends; you get your first boyfriend; you go to college; you start a new job, etc., etc., etc. Once you get out of school, get used to your job, and become accustomed to either being single or in a relationship, it's easy to coast in life. You don't have to learn anything or try something new, so you don't. You go to the same restaurants, hang out with the same friends, and do the same things you've always done. Next thing you know, you wake up one day and realize you're in a full-blown rut. When you get into that position, you get unhappy, you start questioning your choices, and you wonder what went wrong in your life. You do not want to be in that position.

So, how do you avoid it? You read. You listen to audio books. You take seminars. You take classes. You try new things. You learn. You grow.

That doesn't have to stop because you get older, either. In my early forties, for the first time I did a four-mile mud run, ran a half marathon, flipped a 290-pound tire fifty times in a row, started taking jujitsu, got into a negative-two-hundred-degree Cryochamber, walked on hot coals barefoot, traveled to San Francisco and Los Angeles, and went to the Grand Canyon.

What are you going to do for the first time? Learn to draw? Sing karaoke? Give a speech at Toastmasters? Go on a cruise? Learn to cook? Work in a soup kitchen? Feed the homeless? Ride a wave runner? Figure out how to use chopsticks? Go to Yellowstone Park? Learn to shoot? Go bungee jumping? Get a four-hand massage? Learn to box? Dip your toe in the Atlantic and Pacific Oceans? Go paintballing? Ride in a helicopter? Learn a new language? Become a published author? Solve a Rubik's Cube? Do one hundred push-ups in a row? Kiss someone under the mistletoe?

Growing as a human being is kind of like climbing a mountain, and not because you can fall down the side if you don't pay attention to what you're doing. The more you learn and grow, the more the view changes.

Options that never seemed interesting or even possible before suddenly come into focus. Never stop learning. Never stop growing. Do more. Be more. You'll never be sorry.

99. Fame, money, and being remembered are less important than people.

The three abiding desires most people have when they're young are to be rich, to be famous, and to leave a lasting legacy. While none of these things are bad, they're also not as sexy and shiny as they seem.

For example, did you know that studies show people don't get happier after they make $75,000 per year? Once you can pay your bills, have a little left over, and get your basic needs cared for, most people don't get any value out of having even more. Sure, you'd probably enjoy living in that mansion or riding around in your new Rolls Royce for a little while, but after a few weeks, you'd stop being blown away and it wouldn't feel any different than when you had shabbier accommodations. Plus, it may be better to be rich than it is to be poor, but rich people have problems too. They're much more likely to be sued or audited by the IRS. People are always trying to get money out of them; when it's known they're rich, they never know who likes them for themselves and who likes them for their money. Being rich is better than being poor and it gives people a certain degree of freedom and security, but it's not as appealing as it seems.

In our media-driven world where everyone seems to have a brand, fame and celebrity also excite people; however, again, most overrate the appeal of fame. Keep in mind that there are few human beings who become famous enough that even a significant portion of the people they run into recognize them. While fame certainly must seem sweet at first, I doubt if it's as exciting for celebrities when they are being chased by paparazzi, are asked for their hundredth autograph while they are trying to spend some quiet time with their families, or are shouted at by drunken idiots who want to impress their friends by being rude to someone they saw on TV. Meanwhile, it's all so fleeting. The biggest band in the world today may end up only being able to fill a small club in five years. The hot actress may gain ten pounds and be unable to get a role tomorrow. The celebrity who loves being recognized by her fans may find few of them care anymore if her next movie or two bombs. It's fun to be the one everyone is there to see, but as a more famous friend told me later after being mobbed by a gang of picture seekers, it's also dehumanizing because to them you're just someone they've seen on TV. None of those people know or care about you as a human being.

That's the problem most of us face when we want to leave a lasting legacy as well. Many of the great people of an era are completely forgotten after they die, or if they're lucky, their names live on for a decade or two. If you're talking about people like Alexander, Napoleon, Shakespeare, Bach, and Da Vinci, whose names live on through the ages, you're talking about gifted *and* lucky people. Few human beings have their gifts and virtues recognized by more than their immediate family and a few friends. The greatest lovers, the hardest workers, and the most brilliant minds are, for the most part, lost to the ages. The world is like an elephant and we're like ants desperately biting at its feet trying to get it to take a step or two to the side. Rarely do we succeed, and even then, we seldom get it to move far.

Pursue wealth, fame, and fortune if you like, but remember at the end of the day what really matters are your family, your friends, and the people whose hearts you'll be burned into until the day they die. Keep those priorities in order and you'll have a happier life.

100. You're better off spending your money on experiences than things.

It's easy to get obsessed with things: having a house with a view, a new car, a closet full of shoes, a leather couch, an expensive purse, an enormous flat-screen TV, a huge saltwater fish tank, and most importantly, a $3000 massage chair that works your body like a professional massage therapist.

I say "most importantly," because that's the one thing on that list that was important to me. After getting my own house, I wanted to put my own personal stamp on it, and since I love massages, I thought it would be worth it to put some real money into a massage chair. The one I bought is unbelievable. It works every square inch of the back of your body from the soles of your feet all the way up to your neck. It allows you to go "zero gravity" and lean all the way back. It's *amazing* when your back or feet are sore.

However, even though that's my favorite "thing" I've ever bought for myself, buying it wasn't one of my lifetime highlights. When I think back to those moments, they're all experiences.

Walking over hot coals that were north of a thousand degrees, standing around in a minus-190-degree cryogenic chamber in shorts and a T-shirt, seeing the Grand Canyon, going up in a flimsy hot air balloon with low sides that swung every which way if you moved, looking at New York off the top of the Empire State Building, standing on see-through glass near the top of the Sears Tower and looking straight down, finishing a Spartan race, running a half marathon—I could go on, especially if we started getting into dating and being in love.

However, there's no need because the point is that wearing a $1,000 suit and driving a Ferrari may be better than riding around in a beaten-up pickup truck, but when it's all said and done, it'll be the experiences you remember, not the stuff.

It might seem nuts to some people to forego getting a nicer living room set so you can finally visit Hawaii or living in a smaller house than you could otherwise have so that you can always afford to do anything you want to do, but it's the smarter choice. There's a lot to be said for nice things, but they will never make you happy or be as memorable as experiences.

101. Enjoy the moment, because nothing in life is permanent.

I hate to be a downer, but everything good in your life will eventually come to an end. Maybe your soul mate will break up with you, your good friend will drift away, you'll have to put your dog to sleep, your house will burn down, your car will be wrecked, your little boy will grow up and move away.

All of that is setting aside the fact that we are all going to die one day. You, your husband, your parents, your kids—you're going to pass on. I believe those relationships continue on in heaven, but when that death happens, those relationships will end here on earth.

That can either depress you or it can spur you to live in the moment while things are good. Play with your pup, throw the ball around with your kid, enjoy making out with your girlfriend, getting that promotion, or winning a softball game.

Eventually, when that person you love dies, that boyfriend you wanted to marry breaks your heart, or a knee injury keeps you from ever playing volleyball again, it's easy to look back in sorrow at what you've lost. That's the wrong way to think about it. Instead, you should feel gratitude for the good times you had and how they improved your life.

I know what it's like to spend months heartbroken, mooning over a woman who didn't want me anymore. I thought about conversations we had. Daydreamed that things would change. Felt rising anger at her that I forced down because I couldn't hate her for her decision. Eventually, I came to realize it was over, she wasn't coming back, and I had a choice: Either I could let that depress me or I could have gratitude for how much I enjoyed being with her. Once I chose gratitude, all that moping and sadness went away.

Not everyone does that. If you're not careful, you can spend your whole life miserable because you spend all your time thinking about some traumatic event that happened years ago. If that's where you find yourself, you have to tackle the issue so you can move on with your life. Read some books, see a therapist, push yourself to get past it. If you've tried before and it didn't work, then try again.

You only have one life to live, so what are you going to do with it? Are you going to do all those things you've always wanted to do, or are you going to spend your whole life with a case of the "Someday I'll's . . . "? Someday I'll ask that girl out. Someday I'll start that business. Someday I'll learn to draw. Someday I'll go to Las Vegas.

Most of the time, someday is a lot of bullcrap. It's an excuse, a dodge, a way to be lazy. Be one of those people who "seizes the day," and pursue what you want in life now, not in fifty years when you're retired. By then, you should be looking back on a long, happy, productive life, not hoping to finally start living after all this time.

IT'S NOT ALL DOWNHILL

FROM HERE

In my experience with my female friends, it's pretty standard for them to freak out a little bit if they hit thirty and they're not married, and most people, whether they admit it or not, have a bit of a midlife crisis at forty.

That's understandable because, around that age, you figure half your life is over, you're starting to find gray hairs, and that hot young thing you ran across in the supermarket who you're attracted to thinks of you as a "sir" or a "ma'am."

So, what happens when you're too old to go to parties, you're a little too wrinkly to feel comfortable going shirtless at the beach, and you're older than all the people you're seeing on magazine covers? Is it over? Do you sit in your room, gumming hard candy and fuming about "whipper-snappers" until your inevitable hip surgery?

To the contrary, studies consistently show that older Americans are happier than the young. Why wouldn't they be?

Most people are financially better off as they get older. They're more likely to be married. They're less worried about what other people think of them. They're also more likely to already understand all the things you're reading in this book right now.

Believe it or not, you're going to be a different person at fifty than you are right now. You're going to know yourself better, you'll know the world better, and the things that are important to you will change. Can you imagine how much joy you'll get out of spoiling your grandchildren one day? Out of walking into a store and knowing you have the money to buy anything you want? Out of not caring whether the "cool kids" like you or not? Actually, you probably can't imagine it yet, but it'll feel a lot better than you think.

You'll also likely have a lifetime worth of fond memories to look back on, a house full of things you like that you've managed to accumulate over the years, and people you have in your life that you know, like, and trust.

That's something to look forward to, not to dread. Embrace your life, live deeply, and remember that the best years of your life are probably ahead of you.

AUTHOR Q & A

Q: When you graduated high school and were heading off to college, did you have a particular role model in your life that stands out? Whom did you look to for support and advice?

A: I was very lucky to grow up with two grandparents and two parents. That type of love and guidance is priceless. While I appreciated and learned from them, my heroes have always been rebels. Babe Ruth, Muhammad Ali, Jim McMahon, Ayn Rand, Jackie Robinson, Satchel Paige, and Rush Limbaugh all influenced me when I was young.

Q: The advice in 101 Things All Young Adults Should Know *is for new adults in particular, but older, established adults can glean a lot of valuable information from your book. Can you give examples of a couple of pieces of advice that you were given as a new adult that remain with you today?*

A: The single best piece of advice I ever received was "Find something you love so much that you'd do it for free and turn it into a career." I shaped my life around that advice, and it paid off in a huge way.

If I had to pick another, I think I'd go with "If you're not going to remember this five years from now, why worry about it?" I used to have a lot of anxiety when I was young. Now, I can do anything from talking in front of 60,000 listeners on the radio, to sparring, to doing an impromptu speech without getting anxious. Internalizing that advice allows me to just handle it.

Q: Can you explain how your experience growing up formed this book and your advice for new adults?

A: As I mentioned, I grew up with parents and grandparents, and I could ask for advice. I have always been a big reader and have never been afraid to ask successful people questions, but there were still a lot of things I had to learn the hard way. It's not fun to owe $1000 on a credit card when you have no money coming in or to be stuck on the side of the road with a flat tire and unable to change it. So being able to look over the mistakes I made, even with everything I had going for me, helped me know what to talk about in the book.

Q: What do you hope is the most important message young people will take away after finishing your book?

A: If you had to boil it all down, it's all about taking responsibility for yourself. You only get one life and nobody, not your parents, not your friends, not your children, should care as much about it as you do. Accept that getting what you want out of life is on your shoulders and good things will start to slowly but surely happen in your life.

Q: Do you have a favorite piece of advice, perhaps from someone else, that you frequently use in your life?

A: Tony Robbins once said, "Your emotions are nothing but biochemical storms in your brain and you are in control of them at any point in time." A person or situation doesn't make you sad, angry, or upset because you can choose how you react. That doesn't mean there's never a time to feel or display those emotions, but it does mean that if you decide that the emotions you're feeling are unproductive, you can do something about it.

Q: What was your favorite section to write? Can you comment on why it was your favorite?

A: Probably "There's a right time, a right place and a right person to have sex with." Not only is it a fun topic to write about, the reality of it is so completely different from everything you see on TV. I learned that the hard way more than once and it's great to pass on those lessons.

Q: How does it feel to have successfully completed your first book? Do you have others waiting in the wing?

A: I have more than a half dozen full books planned out plus even more relatively short ebooks. The direction I go from here really depends on how well this book does. With that in mind, you should buy five and give them to all your friends.

ABOUT THE AUTHOR

John Hawkins has run his own successful business since 2005 and is one of the most widely read conservative columnists in America. His work regularly appears in *Townhall* and he has also been published in the *Huffington Post*, *Washington Examiner*, *The Hill*, *Human Events*, and *PJ Media*, among many other outlets. His work has been discussed in popular news outlets such as *The Wall Street Journal*, the Rush Limbaugh Show, the Mark Levin Show, Fox, *Newsweek*, *The Washington Post*, ABC News, and CNN. His website, Rightwingnews.com, is one of the biggest conservative websites on the Internet, and his new website defiantmasculinity.com covers issues relating to masculinity and men's rights.

Made in the USA
Columbia, SC
18 January 2021